HEAVY METAL

An ex-Soviet T-54/55 showing turret detail. See page 99

There are few private collectors with the resources to preserve monsters such as this ex-US Marine Corps M103 even if such vehicles were on sale to individuals. See page 83.

HEAVY METAL

CLASSIC ARMOURED FIGHTING VEHICLES IN COLOUR

JOHN BLACKMAN

ARMS AND
ARMOUR

WARRINGTON
BOROUGH
COUNCIL

Arms and Armour Press
A CASSELL IMPRINT
Wellington House, 125 Strand,
London WC2RR 0BB

Distributed in the USA by Sterling Publishing
Co. Inc., 387 Park Avenue South, New York,
NY 10016-8810.

British Library Cataloguing-in-Publication
Data: a catalogue record for this book is available from the British Library

ISBN 1-85409-441-6

Designed and edited by DAG Publications Ltd.
Designed by David Gibbons; layout by
Anthony A. Evans; edited by C. J. Davies;
printed and bound in Italy.

Two British Saladin armoured cars. See page 20.

CONTENTS

INTRODUCTION

The armoured fighting vehicle is past its prime. And if ever evidence were needed to back that controversial statement one need only look at the fact that during the 100 hours of the Gulf War land campaign some 1,300 Iraqi tanks (out of a total of 8,000 vehicles) were destroyed. A sobering thought that needs to be put into some sort of historical perspective.

Tanks were introduced during the First World War in the hope that they would break the deadlock of trench warfare. When a handful of land crabs first crawled out onto the muddy Somme battlefield on 15 September 1916 their impact on that day's fighting was negligible, but then and during subsequent skirmishes valuable lessons were learnt. British Commander-in-Chief Sir Douglas Haig was unconvinced of the tank's worth. But, having exhausted every other plan of action and failed to turn the tide of war in his favour, he was ready to experiment and put the tanks at the forefront of an assault rather than have them play a secondary role to the infantry. At the battle of Cambrai in November 1917 tanks were committed en masse for the first time with nearly 400 tanks leading the assault. Supported by a barrage of machine-gun and artillery fire and followed by infantry, they were intended to punch a hole in the German lines allowing the Cavalry Corps to break through towards the heart of Cambrai. Overhead, aircraft of the Royal Flying Corps would attack enemy targets and report on progress.

Things did not go entirely to plan. The infantry could not keep up with the tanks, bad weather kept aircraft grounded and the cavalry failed to follow through as intended.

Left: A late model Valentine tank in pristine condition. Early models were armed with the inadequate 2pdr anti-tank gun. Late models were gradually upgunned, first with a 6pdr anti-tank gun and finally with a 75mm gun.

Nevertheless the Tank Corps were demonstrably successful in spearheading a potential breakthrough. Warfare would never be the same again. At Cambrai the use of armoured vehicles with following infantry, unregistered artillery fire and air support pointed the way to the future conduct of major land battles for at least the following four decades. While it would be an exaggeration to say that tanks won the First World War they were certainly instrumental in breaking the stalemate and hastening its end.

Between the wars opinions differed as to the value and usage of the tank. The conservative view saw future wars as being relatively static in the fashion of the First World War and favoured the use of the tank as infantry support. Others held that for the armoured fighting vehicle to realise its full potential it should be allowed to operate independently, but in close cooperation with other ground and air arms. Great Britain briefly flirted with the latter approach in the mid to late 1920s with its Experimental Mechanised Force promoted by J. F. C. Fuller, a General Staff Officer who, with hindsight, is judged by many to be the architect of modern tank tactics. The military establishment were unenthusiastic about both Fuller's fervent campaigning and any break from tradition and the project was shelved.

Nevertheless mechanisation was inevitable. The process was not helped by an insistence on 'pigeon-holing' tanks into three categories: light tanks for reconnaissance duties, thinly armoured, fast and armed only with machine-guns; cruiser tanks, fast with heavier armour and firepower (in theory at least) to act as mechanised cavalry and, finally, infantry tanks, slow, heavily armoured and intended, as the category implies, to support infantry. It was almost inevitable that in peacetime, with an unenthusiastic General Staff, what financial resources there were would be concen-

trated on cheaper, light tanks to the detriment of the other two categories. So it was that when war broke out in 1939 Great Britain possessed 1,000 light tanks, but fewer than 150 cruiser and infantry tanks.

Worse still, in none of the categories was firepower put above the other two tenets of tank design, mobility and protection. Nor were there tanks, either in service or development, capable of being up-gunned if ever the need arose. Twin problems which were to afflict British tanks until the closing stages of the Second World War.

Within the German Army, whose senior command had to their detriment all but ignored the tank during the First World War, new ideas and radical theories were easier to embrace and Fuller's preaching did not fall on deaf ears. The terms of the Treaty of Versailles did not allow Germany to maintain a tank force, but by the late 1920s rearmament was underway and there was even a secret testing facility and tank school set up in Russia with the connivance of the Soviet Army. At first Germany produced light tanks under the guise of agricultural tractors, but as Hitler came to power rearmament became an open fact. At least for those that wanted to see it. By 1935 Germany had three panzer divisions, one of which was commanded by General Heinz Guderian. Guderian, a tank man through and through, was deeply influenced by Fuller and had his own similar theories. But unlike Fuller, who was all but ostracised in Britain, Guderian had Hitler's full support and resources were directed into producing a panzer force without par.

While the rest of Europe was inclined towards defence, Guderian and his contemporaries were refining their so called 'Blitzkrieg' tactics; lightning strikes deep into enemy territory spearheaded by armour and supported by motorised infantry and airpower. When Germany invaded Poland on 1 September 1939 the Wehrmacht, like the British Army, had a

Above: The remains of an M2 half-track await restoration.
Below: It is hard to believe that this weed infested hulk will be returned to a good-as-new Priest self-propelled gun in the fullness of time.

universal tank – the Centurion being a good example. Post-war, as relations between NATO and the Soviet Bloc dropped to freezing point, technology advanced to the point where designers could balance fire-power, mobility and protection without trading one off against the other to a detrimental extent. The result was the devastatingly capable main battle tank (MBT). Nevertheless tank design has been development- rather than innovation-led. For innovation we have to look to the skies. The modern armoured fighting vehicle has become just another weapon in an army's arsenal. Faster, better armoured and packing a mightier punch than ever before, but no different in concept from the land crabs that appeared on the Somme in 1916. On the other hand, airborne weaponry has advanced beyond all recognition with the result that, on today's battlefield, armour has no place to run, no place to hide.

It is the success of the AFV that has been its undoing. Post-war on both sides of the Iron Curtain a lot of effort went into the development of new, more efficient anti-tank weapons with the result that where once the armoured fighting vehicle was often the predator it is now all too frequently the prey. Against sophisticated mines, guns and missiles – particularly air launched missiles – the AFV has little meaningful defence. Of course armour is far from redundant. Air superiority may be the key to winning many a future conflict, but aircraft cannot hold territory. There must be a military presence on the ground. So, as far as one can tell, there will always be a need for the armoured fighting vehicle even if it is no longer likely to be delivering the decisive blow.

Despite airborne technology having effectively ended the AFV's reign over the battlefield, fascination for these muscle-bound machines is undiminished. Post-Second World War and, to a lesser extent post-Cold War, surplus soft-skin military vehicles found a ready civilian market among companies and individuals looking for utilitarian workhorses. Therefore relatively large numbers have survived redundancy, albeit frequently modified for secondary careers with farmers, garages,

preponderance of light tanks. But by the time they advanced on the Low Countries in May 1940 and further afield to North Africa in February 1941, the light PzKpfw Is and IIs were quickly being phased out and replaced by the excellent PzKpfw IIIs and IVs which, unlike their British counterparts, were capable of being up-gunned. From then until the end of the war it has to be concluded that German tank designs were generally a step, or even two, ahead of British and

American designs. The Allies, with the exception of the Soviets who jumped straight to the top of the class with their T-34, were forced to play a continuous game of 'catch-up'. Fortunately the Allies had the industrial capacity to produce many thousands of armoured vehicles and make up for design shortcomings by sheer weight of numbers.

By the end of the war all sides seemed to be heading towards the concept of a

Above: Filling the tank of an M5 Stuart.
Below: One of the biggest problems associated with owning armour is moving it!

haulage contractors and the like. In comparison the civilian market for surplus armoured vehicles is tiny – or at least it was until the current surge of interest from military vehicle collectors. Half-tracks have frequently been stripped of their armour and converted to perform heavy duty civilian tasks. But to what purpose can a tank or self-propelled gun be put other than to that for which it was designed?

Until relatively recently with the exception of a few examples retained by museums, most surplus armour was either sold for scrap or used for target practice. Either way an ignominious end. Therefore, compared with the number of ex-military soft-skin vehicles extant there were few armoured fighting vehicles preserved for posterity. That is no longer the case. Armour has become a collectible. It was inevitable that soft-skin military vehicle enthusiasts would eventually turn their attention

towards armour. But had a successful UK businessman and enthusiast named Tony Budge not purchased an ex-Portuguese Army M4 and Sexton in December 1983 things might have been very different. Budge was bitten by the armour bug and, having the wherewithal, set about building the biggest tank collection in the world. Within ten years the Budge Collection had more vehicles than the Bovington Tank Museum, and more importantly, they were all in running condition.

Budge's acquisition team, headed by Bob Fleming, scoured the world in search of rare and interesting vehicles (or heaps of scrap that had once been rare and interesting vehicles!) which could be shipped back to the UK for restoration. Unfortunately the Budge holding company collapsed in 1993 and virtually the entire collection was sold off, but their activities had by then inspired others to begin collecting and restoring. Few could afford to scour an Australian scrapyard for bits of a Matilda to satisfy their urge to own a tank, but with the removal of the Iron Curtain and the resulting downsizing of armies, fleets of armour had suddenly become surplus to requirements on both sides of the old East/West divide. And more to the point, it was for sale. Anyone could buy, directly or via a dealer, almost anything from an armoured personnel carrier to a Chieftain MBT. With armour available from the hard currency starved ex-Eastern Bloc and from European NATO members disposing of surplus stock, the market was all but flooded. Apparently there are now more armoured fighting vehicles in private hands in the UK than are owned by the British Army. Just as well then that all guns must be certified deactive.

Use the word restoration in connection with say, vintage cars, and you'll probably imagine a nuts and bolts strip down and rebuild to concours standard. All glittering chrome and polished paintwork. Notwithstanding a marked lack of chrome and polished paintwork, most of the vehicles featured in this book have undergone painstaking ground-up rebuilds. Particularly the older vehicles. In fact – and this is a sweeping generalisation and therefore almost certainly unfair – the older the

vehicle the more likely it is to have been restored to good as new condition. Much of the modern armour you'll see has been restored to running order, but looks as if it has just come out of battle. The reason is obvious when you think about it. Vintage armour is too rare and valuable to be driven hard whereas more up-to-date equipment can be thrashed as the designers intended. Collectors don't generally buy a Chieftain as an ornament and parts are available in the event of something breaking. Almost all the vehicles featured in 'Heavy Metal' are in running order. The few that are not, for instance the infamous Tiger I, are included because of their importance in an historical context.

The upsurge of interest in armour over the past 10 to 15 years has also proved a shot in the arm for museums. As in other fields of vehicle preservation, be it steam locomotives, traction engines, or vintage aircraft, a considerable amount of a museum's restoration work is undertaken by volunteers. The symbiotic relationship between that Mecca for the armour enthusiast, the Imperial War Museum, and the Duxford Aviation Society's Vehicle Wing

may not be typical, but it illustrates how such arrangements can benefit all parties involved – including the general public. The Vehicle Wing consists of some 40–50 volunteers and is primarily tasked by the Imperial War Museum (IWM) with the job of restoring and maintaining its collection of armoured vehicles. Some 15 to 20 years ago, when the IWM collection was a fraction of the size it is now, the volunteers spent the vast majority of their time doing just that, and fitting in work on their own few softskin vehicles as and when they could. There were hardly any privately owned AFVs at that time. Now that the IWM collection has grown enormously and moved into hi-tech, purpose-built accommodation where the vehicles are displayed in diorama settings, there has been a complete change of emphasis. The volunteers find that most of their time is now spent working on armour either on loan to, or owned by, themselves.

There are three main reasons for the change. Firstly, the IWM is no different from any other museum in that it has neither the space nor budget voraciously to acquire everything it might like. Secondly, there are plenty of armoured vehicles around of

Above: The older an AFV is the more likely it is to be maintained in pristine condition and treated with kid gloves.

interest to enthusiasts and public alike, but which are strictly speaking outside the IWM's sphere of interest and probably wouldn't be acquired for their collection even if budget and space were available. Thirdly, armour of almost any shape, size and age can now be bought by anyone. So, with the IWM's agreement, the Vehicle Wing collect vehicles that are either on the periphery of the IWM's collection policy or that make good back-ups for the main collection. The result is that the IWM collection is kept pristine (bar the odd splash of mud for realism) in the Land Warfare Hall, while outside sit rows of more modern armour, most of which is owned by the Vehicle Wing. And in the workshops a Cromwell tank, recovered for the IWM collection from a Salisbury Plain firing range some years ago, is worked on next to a volunteer's personal Humber Pig. Everyone benefits. The Imperial War Museum has the voluntary manpower necessary to maintain most of their collec-

Above: Modern armour, such as these two Chieftains, is likely to have almost as hard a life in private hands as in service.

tion in working order, Vehicle Wing members get access to excellent workshop facilities, and the public get to see twice as many vehicles as they would otherwise.

What does the future hold for the armoured vehicle collector and enthusiast? That's hard to say. Public interest is higher than it has ever been. In 1997 some 18,000 paying members of the general public attended the War & Peace Show organised by the UK's Invicta Military Vehicle Preservation Society. True, with over 2,000 military vehicles on show it is the biggest and best of its kind in the world, but clearly they are attracting non-enthusiast members of the public who are simply looking for a good day out. An unlikely situation a decade ago when events were geared up for the vehicle owners themselves and a far cry from the widely promoted and professionally run (albeit by amateurs!) War & Peace Show.

The number of individuals owning armour has increased enormously over the past five years, as has the supply of available armour. Up until three or four years ago when the UK Ministry of Defence (MOD) wanted to dispose of surplus armour it invited tenders from vetted dealers. Those with the right firearms licence could take away their purchases 'as is', those without had to pay for guns to be deactivated. There was also a clause in the purchase contract to the effect that if a buyer subsequently wanted to sell a vehicle the MOD had to be informed so that the next prospective purchaser could be vetted. A difficult clause to enforce. Next the MOD tried auctioning surplus vehicles, but apparently that was not particularly financially rewarding. Now rumour has it that the MOD will no longer be selling surplus vehicles to private dealers and collectors. Instead most will be consigned to the smelting pot.

From the end of the Second World War until the mid-fifties the US Army disposed of surplus armour to scrap dealers and their yards were happy hunting grounds for collectors looking for vehicles and parts. Large numbers of Second World War vintage AFVs were also left behind in Europe to re-equip those allied armies who had no vehicle stocks of their own. Many of these vehicles have since been sold off, but, unfortunately for the AFV collector, under the original terms of the military aid programmes under which they were supplied the receiving country had to agree to 'fully demilitarise and render unserviceable' any armour they subsequently sold. Some countries seem to have enforced that clause more rigorously than others, but the end result for many a buyer has been an armour plate jigsaw.

In recent years those vehicles which the US Army could not sell or pass on to friendly governments were generally melted down or presented to museums and veterans' organisations. At least one M60 was delivered to a veterans' organisation in running condition. The vets jump-started it and had a whale of a time before the Army came back and welded all the hatches shut! Surplus M60 MBTs have even been dumped off the East Coast of America to act as artificial reefs. The US Army is also empowered to swap armour with museums and private collectors in return for a rare vehicle that an Army museum particularly wants to acquire and cannot afford to buy, but otherwise any

collector who wants modern US armour in his collection is going to have to wait a long time. Lack of access to modern US armour accounts for an increase in interest from American collectors in British AFVs which are, for the time being at least, freely available and reasonably priced.

Despite uncertainties the vehicle market is extremely buoyant, as one look at the 'for sale' ads in the enthusiast press will testify. It's also said that there are still plenty of hulks lying forgotten on ranges awaiting recovery. With permission of course. In 1997 a group of men in the United States were taken to court for allegedly stealing derelict vehicles and parts from an Army range. And the old Eastern Bloc countries are as willing as ever to exchange heavy metal for hard currency. So it is likely that supply will still be able to meet an increasing demand. Armoured fighting vehicles will never attract the following of vintage cars or steam locomotives, they don't have the same aesthetic appeal. But for those who appreciate pure mechanical power without ornament or frippery, there is nothing quite like 'Heavy Metal'.

Acknowledgements

My sincere thanks go to all the AFV owner/operators and enthusiasts who have generously allowed me to photograph their vehicles and/or supplied photographic material from their own collections, in particular Bob Fleming, Rex and Rod Cadman, Andy Hutcheson, Fraser Gray, Mark Ansell, Hans Halberstadt, Nigel Hay, Frank Buck and Ralf Thiel, Director of the Panzermuseum, Münster. And, lest I unwittingly smear the reputations of any of the aforementioned, let me make it clear that all errors or omissions are entirely mine.

I am also grateful to the Imperial War Museum, Duxford, and the Tank Museum, Bovington, for allowing me the special privilege of photographing their fine collections in action and reproducing the results, and to the Invicta Military Vehicle Preservation Society for their wholehearted cooperation.

All photographs were taken by the author unless otherwise credited.

Top left: Whatever the future holds for the AFV in service, fascination for these muscle-bound machines remains undiminished and the public flock to events such as the incomparable annual show organised by the Imperial War Museum's Vehicle Wing at Duxford.
Lower left: Rip-roaring, mud-slinging action from the Imperial War Museum's Conqueror.
Right: Any AFV display is enhanced enormously by the participants dressing the part.

UNITED KINGDOM

Morris Light Reconnaissance Car

During the Second World War Morris Motors Ltd produced 2,050 light reconnaissance cars. They were powered by Morris's own 71bhp four-cylinder engine and had a top speed of 50mph. The armour was 14mm thick and protected the three-man crew from small calibre fire only. The Mk I, of which 1,000 were manufactured, was rear wheel drive and had an independent coil spring front suspension, but the Mk II had four-wheel drive and a rigid front axle with leaf-springs. Both marks were armed with a Boys anti-tank rifle and a Bren gun.

Restored vehicles are frequently displayed for charitable purposes or at commemorative events. This painstakingly rebuilt and detailed Mk II Morris Light Reconnaissance Car (**right**) was photographed during the 'Tribute and Promise' parade in The Mall in August 1995. It was originally built in October 1944 but was never commissioned. When discovered by a vehicle dealer in a Dorset barn it only had 264 miles on the clock but was seized solid and in a very dilapidated condition. The current owner fell in love with it 'rust and all' and bought it. Months of work later he had the engine running and the gearbox

working, but the clutch was still stubbornly seized. Taking the bull by the horns the owner forced the Morris into gear and proceeded to drive it deliberately into the stump of an elm tree. The impact did little or no damage to either party but it did free the clutch! Since then the elderly Morris has sedately covered 800 miles about which the owner says, 'It starts, stops, steers in the

right direction – although it leans alarmingly when cornering – what more could I ask?'

Humber Mk III Light Reconnaissance Car

Humber built a series of light reconnaissance cars on the chassis of their Humber Super Snipe car. With the exception that the Mk I (known as Ironside I) was open-topped and the Mks II and III were enclosed, all three marks had similar body shells of 12mm thick armour plate. The Mk II was armed with a .55 calibre Boys anti-tank rifle mounted to the left of the driver and had a Bren light machine-gun mounted on the roof protected by a semi-circular shield. The Mk III emerged in 1943 and was fitted with a full-blown turret for the Bren and had the added advantage of four-wheel drive.

The 87bhp six-cylinder Humber engine gave the three-ton Mk III a top speed of a little over 40mph. some 3,600 of all marks were built and they served with army reconnaissance units and the Royal Air Force, as the restored vehicle pictured on the move (**left**, courtesy of Mark Ansell) illustrates.

The other vehicle (**right**) presents something of a puzzle because it is open-topped, but, since it has four-wheel drive, is clearly based on a Mk III chassis. Unfortunately the current owner knows nothing of the vehicle's history. The markings are those of the 49th (West Riding) Division as worn in North Western Europe.

Daimler Dingo

Best known and loved British scout car is undoubtedly the Daimler Dingo. The vehicle was the result of an invitation made in 1938 to Daimler, Alvis and BSA to submit designs for a turretless scout car. The BSA design was judged the best and, after modifications including the addition of a roof, taken over by Daimler for production. The diminutive Dingo is only 10ft 5in long, 4ft 11in high and weighs a little over three tons. All of the 6,626 Dingos produced had four-wheel drive, but the Mk I, which entered production in 1939, also had four-wheel steering, an innovative feature which proved both unpopular and unsafe and was therefore dropped from the Mk II onwards.

The thinly armoured octagonal hull only offered protection from small calibre fire and was quite a tight fit for the two-man crew (**right**). The commander's left-hand seat swivelled to give him an all round view and easy access to the two radios carried at the rear of the crew compartment. The driver's seat, which could be raised or lowered, was set an angle to make it easier to reverse the Dingo out of trouble while looking through the rear hatch. The 55hp Daimler six-cylinder engine is rear-mounted and drives through a single speed transfer box and differential. Five forward and five reverse gears allow the Dingo to advance or retreat at speeds up to 55mph. Armament was usually restricted to a single Bren gun fired through a port at the front plus the crew's personal arms.

Ford in Canada produced an almost identical vehicle known as the Lynx Mk II between 1942 and 1945. Both the Dingo and Lynx served well beyond the Second World War. Some saw action with UN Forces in Korea and many were handed down to Third World armies. The Dingo Mk II illustrated (**right**) was built in 1943 and bears the

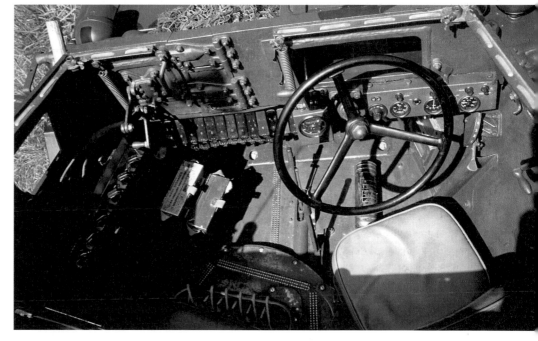

white mailed gauntlet marking of the 6th Armoured Division who were particularly active during the Italian campaign. It also bears the insignia of the King's Royal Rifles circa 1954 with whom the vehicle's current owner once served. In fact it was on a Dingo that he learned to drive so, as is often the case, his choice of a restoration project has an element of sentiment. The vehicle's engine is remarkably quiet and, despite being over 50 years old and solidly mounted to the chassis, exhibits not a trace of vibration – a tribute to Daimler engineering. Note that although this vehicle appears to have once had an armoured roof, in common with most surviving Dingos, the roof has at some stage been replaced by a canvas cover. Apparently 'tin-tops' were about as popular as four-wheel steering. The Dingo served in most theatres including the Western Desert as typified by the sand-coloured Dingo (**left**) bearing the badge of the 22nd Armoured Brigade who served in the Western Desert with Eighth Army.

Humber Mk I Scout Car

When it looked as if Daimler/BSA could not produce enough Dingos to meet demand, the Rootes Group were asked to design and manufacturer a similar vehicle. The resulting Humber Mk I armoured car appeared in 1942 and utilised many components already being used in existing Humber 4x4 vehicles. At 12ft 7in long it was larger than the Dingo and could accommodate a three-man crew, but since the Humber Mk I's armour was marginally thinner the vehicle was only slightly heavier than its Daimler contemporary. However, it was fitted with an engine capable of developing over 50% more horsepower than the Dingo's and was therefore able to achieve an impressive 62mph top speed with a range of about 200 miles. It was generally armed with a single Bren or Vickers-Berthier machine-gun. Some 4,300 were built, but restored vehicles (**left**) are relatively rare.

Daimler Mk I and II Armoured Car

The Daimler Mk I armoured car (**top right**), which was developed in 1940 and put into service in 1941, is effectively a larger version of the Dingo scout car with a turret added. In fact the turret and its 2pdr gun (**above**) (with a Besa 7.92mm machine-gun mounted coaxially) was based on that used by the Tetrarch light tank. The Mk II (**overleaf top**) featured several improvements including a modified gun mounting, more efficient radiator and a driver's

escape hatch. The Daimler six-cylinder 95hp engine gave both versions a maximum road speed of 50mph and a range of about 200 miles. An unusual feature was the inclusion of a second, rearward facing, driving position.

The Daimler Mk I and improved Mk II were the most advanced British armoured cars of the Second World War combining as they did the armour protection and firepower of a light tank with a high performance, four-wheel drive chassis. Some 2,700 were finally produced and they saw service in most theatres.

Humber Mk IV Armoured Car

The Humber Mk IV was introduced in 1942 and was the last of a line of armoured cars produced by the Rootes Group during the Second World War based on their Karrier KT4 artillery tractor. Early marks had all been armed with a 15mm main gun, but the Mk IV (**lower left**, courtesy of Fraser Gray) mounted a much improved 37mm gun of American design. All marks had a coaxial 7.92mm Besa.

The six-cylinder 90hp engine was rear mounted and drove either the rear or all four wheels via a four-speed gearbox and two-speed transfer box. The Humber Mk IV had a top speed of about 45mph and a range approaching 250 miles.

Ferret Mk 1 and Mk 2

The Ferret is very popular among AFV collectors and readily available. The turretless Ferret Mk 1 prototype appeared in 1949 and both the Mk 1 (**top right**) and turreted Mk 2 went into production in 1952. Ferret production continued until 1971 with 4,400 eventually being produced, many of which were exported. The original Mk 1 was designed as a three-man, open-top scout car to replace the venerable Dingo and was armed with only a light machine-gun. The Mk 2 was equipped with a manually traversed turret in which was mounted a .30 calibre Browning, but had a crew of only two. A Ferret's armour does not exceed ½in thickness and they weigh in at about four tons. They are powered by a reliable six cylinder 4,258cc Rolls-Royce engine driving all wheels via a five-speed (forward and reverse) pre-select

gearbox and are capable of a maximum road speed approaching 60mph. As armoured cars go Ferrets make relatively practical road-going vehicles. However, visibility is poor and a 'commander' in the turret is almost essential.

The Ferret Mk 2/3 illustrated (**below**) was purchased in very poor condition from a farmer who had used it for towing duties. Several layers of peeling paint had to be painstakingly chipped off and many missing or rusted parts replaced. Luckily Ferret spares are plentiful if not always cheap. Enquiries reveal that the vehicle was built in 1960, served first in Cyprus and then in Northern Ireland where it was blast

damaged in 1975. It was returned to England and kept in store until sold as surplus. The other Ferret illustrated (**above**) is also a Mk 2/3 but actually started life as a fixed turret Mk 1/2 and was converted during restoration.

There were a number of special-purpose variants created during the Ferret's long

production life. The Mk 2/6 had Vigilant missile launchers located on either side of its turret while the Mk 5 had Swingfires. There was even an amphibious version, the Mk 3, fitted with a flotation screen and larger wheels which propelled the vehicle at a stately 2mph in calm waters. Ferrets last saw action with the British Army during the Gulf War (**left**) and have now been withdrawn from service.

Saladin FV601

Developed alongside the Saracen APC, both designs drew heavily on experience gained during the war. The prototype Saladin appeared in 1953 and after a protracted development programme the type finally entered service with the British Army in 1958. Weighing about ten tons and armed with an L5A1 76.2mm rifled gun, the Saladin must rank as one of the most impressive vehicles it is possible to drive on the street with any degree of ease (**top right**). The driver sits in the centre of the front hull and has an inverted power assisted steering wheel and five gears in both forward and reverse at his command. The gunner and commander occupy the turret which can be traversed electrically or manually. Saladin shares the same chassis as the Saracen

armoured personnel carrier and is powered by a Rolls-Royce B80 No 1 Mk 6D eight-cylinder engine with drive to all six wheels, the front four of which steer. Maximum road speed is in the region of 45mph with a range of about 250 miles.

Before production ceased in 1972 some 1,177 Saladins had been manufactured and it sold quite well on the export market with examples going to West Germany, the Far East and Africa. In British Army service they were last used in Cyprus and by Territorial Army units. Now that they have been withdrawn completely and replaced by the Scorpion, several have found their way into private collections.

Saracen FV603

Armoured half-track personnel carriers were used extensively by both sides during the Second World War, but being open-topped did not offer much protection to their passengers. With that in mind the post-war British Army demanded a fully enclosed armoured personnel carrier. The Alvis Saracen (**right**) was the result. Its box-like welded steel hull could accommodate ten infantrymen plus driver and vehicle commander. The latter occupied the small, .30 calibre Browning machine-gun armed, manually traversable turret. There were also three gun ports in either side of the hull through which onboard troops could fire their personal weapons.

The Saracen APC was developed at the same time as the Saladin armoured car and

shares the same chassis and drivetrain. All six wheels are driven by the Rolls-Royce B80 5,675cc engine via a five-speed pre-selector gearbox. The suspension was quite sophisticated for its day and features a fully independent double wishbone system. Saracen has hydraulically assisted steering on the front four wheels and hydraulic brakes on all six.

Saracen went into production in 1952, earlier than Saladin, because the British Army had a greater need for APCs as a result of their involvement in policing actions in Malaya. Like Saladin, Saracen sold well overseas, going to Jordan, Nigeria, Kuwait and Australia among others. Production ceased in 1972. Saracen was gradually being retired from front-line British Army service when the fully tracked FV432 came on the scene in the sixties, but disturbances in Northern Ireland gave it a new sense of purpose. Large numbers were taken out of store and shipped to Ulster where they were gradually up-armoured and fitted with CS gas or smoke dischargers. By 1984 they were no longer needed in Ulster and either placed in store or relegated to training duties. Many have since been sold off to

collectors although the blue Saracen illustrated (**above**) served for a while with the Hong Kong police before being pensioned off.

Humber Pig FV1611

Despite rushing the Alvis Saracen into service in the mid-fifties the British Army were still short of APCs and as a stop-gap measure had Humber build a utilitarian vehicle based on an already existing four-wheel drive truck chassis. The result was officially designated FV1611 and about 1,700 were manufactured between 1955 and 1959. The ugly box-like hull accommodated eight infantrymen plus a driver and commander. The vehicle was only lightly armoured and had no armament of its own, although there were firing ports in the hull and rear doors. Several variants were produced including an ambulance and a command and control vehicle.

In the 1960s as the combination of Saracen and FV432 production started to meet the British Army's needs so the Humbers were put into store or sold as surplus. However, escalating problems in Northern Ireland prompted the British

Government to take out of store or purchase back from civilian owners as many of the old FV1611s as they could and ship them to Ulster as patrol vehicles. When it was realised in 1972 that the IRA had armour-piercing rounds that could penetrate the vehicle's armour, all 500 or so still serving in Ulster were returned to Royal Ordnance Factories in the UK for up-armouring under Operation 'Bracelet'. They also received suspension modifications to cope with the extra weight which, in truth, took the Humber's chassis and drivetrain up to and beyond its practical limits. Thereafter there could be no doubt that the FV1611's nickname of 'Pig' was truly a reflection of its looks, handling and driveability.

The well-worn blue Pig illustrated (**top right**) went on to serve with London's Metropolitan Police before being purchased by its current owners who use it to transport members of the public to and from a tank driving course. At the other end of the restoration scale is this prize-winning 1953-built example (**centre right**). It entered service with the British Army in January 1954. Between then and its going to Northern Ireland in 1971 nothing is known

of the vehicle's history. After serving with various regiments in Northern Ireland the Pig was made surplus in 1992. The current owner has returned the vehicle to tip-top condition and removed some of the internal armour plate. However, he reports that it still drives like a pig.

Hornet

More an oddity than a classic is this Humber Hornet preserved by the Tank Museum, Bovington. The official designation is 'FV1620, truck, 1 ton, armoured launcher, 4x4 Humber', and it is basically a Humber Pig modified to mount a pair of Australian made Malkara wire-guided anti-tank missiles. The HESH (High-Explosive Squash Head) missile had a range of 4,000 metres and could destroy any known tank of its era.

Only 24 were constructed in the early 'sixties and this survivor (**bottom left**) bears the markings of Cyclops Squadron of the 2nd Royal Tank Regiment which formed part of the Strategic Reserve in the 3rd Division. Hornets were replaced by Ferret Mk 5s armed with Swingfire missiles in 1969.

Land Rover ½ ton Utility

This (**overleaf top**) must be about the only armoured vehicle that a collector could drive to the supermarket with any degree of practicality. It is, in military nomenclature, a Land Rover, Truck, Utility, ½ ton, fitted with a Northern Ireland Vehicle Protection Kit (VPK). This particular vehicle was built in February 1974 and sold off as surplus from the vehicle sub-depot at Holywood in Northern Ireland in May 1993. Nothing is known of its service life other than was discovered when stripping off layers of paint. In among the coats of NATO green and black, NATO green and bronze green was discovered the badge of 39th Infantry Brigade which was known to have covered the Belfast area. Also, at some stage it had been fitted with a substantial roll cage, probably for protection against the effects of culvert mines. The Vehicle Protection Kit, fitted to most Land Rovers serving in Northern Ireland, consisted of glass reinforced plastic panels known as 'Makrolon' armour, which afforded the crew reasonable protection against blast, some small-arms

fire, Claymore mines, nail and petrol bombs etc. Fitting a VPK was supposed to take 35 man hours and it could be just as easily (?) stripped off and used on another vehicle.

At present the only such vehicle in private hands, 16 FM 81, is painted to represent a vehicle in service during the early to mid 1980s. The VPK was acquired separately via the MOD and the owner comments that it took a lot longer to fit than the 35 man hours specified. Close examination of the vehicle reveals signs of burning under both wings and the underside indicating that it has been on the receiving end of a petrol bomb attack at least once.

Fox

The Fox (**centre left and below**) was designed by Daimler as a successor to the Ferret in the reconnaissance role. Manufacture was undertaken by the Royal Ordnance Factory in Leeds and the first production vehicle came off the line in 1973. It was intended to be a considerable improvement over its predecessor, and so it was, but it was also considerably more expensive to manufacture so only a few hundred were built before the assembly line closed in 1986. A turretless liaison version known as Vixen, did not even go into production although two pre-production models survive in working order (**top right**).

Although intended to directly replace the Ferret, the three-man Fox is larger and

design and a tendency to oversteer. Army drivers were given corrective training, but it is a potential problem that civilian drivers need to be aware of.

Vickers Medium Mk II

The Vickers Medium (**below**) was the first British tank in service to feature a revolving gun turret and sprung suspension and was the Royal Tank Corps' standard tank from 1923 until the late thirties. The Mk I was introduced in 1923 and followed by the Mk II in 1925. They shared the same Quick Firing 3pdr gun, chassis and engine, but the Mk II had thicker armour, a slightly modified superstructure and a different steering mechanism known as Rackham Steering. In addition to the 3pdr the Mk II was armed with two Vickers machine-guns in the hull sides and three Hotchkiss machine-guns protruding from the turret. Vickers Mediums were powered by a 90bhp Armstrong-Siddeley V8 engine which gave the 13-ton tank a top speed of about 15mph and a range of 150 miles.

almost 50% heavier. It was constructed from aluminium rather than steel armour and armed with a hard-hitting 30mm Rarden cannon capable of firing either single shots or six-round bursts. Night-vision devices and flotation screens were fitted as standard. A militarised Jaguar 4,200cc engine drives all four wheels via fluid couplings, and a pre-select gearbox offers the driver

five forward and five reverse gears. Fox is capable of 65mph on the road and had an operating range of close to 250 miles. The Jaguar engine is easy enough to work on and the Fox is becoming quite popular with AFV collectors. One word of warning however. During its first few years of service the Fox was involved in some serious accidents because of its top-heavy

In 1932 two modified Mk IIs were introduced; the Mk II*, which had a single

Vickers coaxial machine-gun in place of the three Hotchkiss guns and the commander's cupola moved further back on the turret roof, and the Mk II** which had an armoured radio container added to the turret rear. In total 160 Vickers Mediums were built and they played an important part in training and tactical experimentation between the wars . It is thought that none saw action in British Army service although it is believed that some of the 15 purchased by the Russians for training may have been used in combat on the Finnish Front in 1941.

The vehicle illustrated (**previous page**, courtesy of Mark Ansell) is a Mk II* which was restored to running order by Vickers Defence Systems during the early eighties and presented to the Tank Museum, Bovington.

Universal Carrier

The Universal Carrier can trace its origins back to the mid-thirties when the British Army dabbled with a number of small, tracked armoured vehicles intended to tow guns or carry personnel. In 1936 the Carrier Machine Gun No 1 Mk I went into service. It carried a crew of three in its open-topped body constructed from 10mm thick armour and was armed with a Vickers .303 machine-gun. The Carrier Machine Gun No 2 Mk II which had a Bren gun instead of the Vickers appeared in 1937 and, in 1938, a whole range of carriers appeared specifically built for such purposes as mounting a 3in smoothbore gun and observation duties.

The carriers were popular and much in demand, but it did not make economic or practical sense to build a range of different versions for specific purposes. Therefore in 1940 a new vehicle was introduced, the Universal Carrier No 1 Mk I, which could be adapted for any purpose with the addition of a factory installed modification kit. The basic Universal Carrier weighed between 4 and 4½ tons and had an open-topped body constructed of riveted armour plate of between 7 and 10mm thick. Armament usually consisted of a Bren gun and a Boys anti-tank rifle. The rear-mounted engine was a Ford V8 driving the rear axle via a four-speed gearbox. Top speed on good going could be as high as 30mph. The driver steered via a conventional steering wheel which caused the tracks to 'warp' by laterally moving the front bogie assemblies and, for tighter turns, applied the brakes to one or the other track.

Despite the Universal Carrier being built in Britain by Thornycroft, Ford, Morris and others, UK production was unable to satisfy demand so they were also manufactured in Australia, New Zealand, Canada and the United States. Among the roles for which the carrier could be adapted were: observation post, flame-thrower, mortar carrier, ambulance, anti-aircraft gun carrier and machine-gun carrier. The vehicle illustrated (**below**), a Universal Carrier Mk III manufactured in 1943, is armed with a Vickers medium machine-gun (**right**) affixed to a tripod mount behind the driver.

Mk I Infantry Tank

Hardly a classic in the true sense of the word, it could be said that the Mk I Infantry Tank's saving grace was that it at least pointed the way not to go in the future. While the German High Command realised that mobility was to be a key factor in any future war, in Britain senior opinion imag-

60mm thick. This rare survivor (**below**) is maintained in working order by the Tank Museum at Bovington in Dorset from where it makes occasional forays to military vehicle shows.

Matilda II

In truth the Infantry Tank Mk I was introduced as a cheap interim measure while development progressed on the Infantry Tank Mk II (or A12) which, when the Mk I was retired after Dunkirk, officially inherited the name Matilda. Although the name was the same, the Matilda II was a completely different animal. Design work started in 1936 with the intention of producing a tank capable of 15mph and armed with a 2pdr gun and a coaxially mounted 7.92mm Besa machine-gun. The Vulcan Foundry in Warrington had produced mock-ups by April 1937 and, after various engine layouts had been considered, it was decided to install twin AEC six-cylinder diesels matched to a Wilson epicyclic gearbox.

ined that any future European war was likely to be fought along the lines of the 1914–18 conflict and therefore favoured the use of the tank as infantry support. The Infantry Tank Mk I, or A11 as it was designated, was perhaps one of the worst results of this outdated concept, being little more than a mobile machine-gun post.

The project commenced in 1935 under the security code name 'Matilda' because, so legend has it, of the vehicle's comical duck-like appearance. Only 140 were built and the type saw action in France in 1940 where, inevitably, its top speed of 8mph and single .303 Vickers machine-gun armament proved unsatisfactory despite armour up to

In December 1937, before the pilot A12 was even ready, an order was placed 'off the

drawing board' for 65 tanks – increased in May the following year to 165. The hull was constructed by bolting together armour plates and castings through tapped holes, and the tracks were protected by one-piece armour skirts inset with five mud chutes. In fact the design was less than ideal from a mass production point of view and only two were in service when war broke out. In May 1940 two dozen Infantry Tank Mk IIs were shipped to France along with a similar number of Mk Is. They had some initial success when, near Arras, they attacked the flanks of Rommel's motorised infantry regiments and the SS Division Totenkopf. Light anti-tank weapons deployed against them had no effect on the Mk II's thick armour and the chaos that the attack caused gained the British Expeditionary Force much-needed time to prepare for evacuation. The story was a similar one when the 7th Royal Tank Regiment were shipped with their Matilda IIs to Egypt in August 1940. The Matilda II's armour, up to 78 mm thick on the hull front, proved almost immune to Italian anti-tank and tank fire during the early months of the Western Desert campaign. These were possibly the Matilda's finest hours because once the

German Afrika Korps came on the scene in mid-1941 and employed their 88mm anti-aircraft guns in an anti-tank role the Matilda II proved as vulnerable as any other vehicle.

When first introduced the Matilda II was perhaps the most formidable tank in service. Almost 3,000 were produced and they served with the British, Australian and Russian armies. Unfortunately a major shortcoming was that the Matilda's small

turret ring precluded 'up-gunning' and as heavier firepower and armour took to the battlefield so it was relegated to being used as the basis for a range of special-purpose vehicles (including various mine clearing variants) until production ceased in August 1943. Illustrated (**above**) is a Mk IV which is awaiting restoration to running condition after being recovered from Australia where many Matildas ended up after becoming

obsolete in the European and North African theatres. The fully restored vehicle in standard 1940–41 desert camouflage (**bottom left and right**, courtesy of Hans Halberstadt) is ex-Budge Collection now owned by US collector Jacques Littlefield.

Infantry Tank Mk III Valentine

The Valentine (**below**) was designed by Vickers-Armstrong's as a private venture. Popular legend has it that the name Valentine was adopted because the design was submitted to the War Office on St Valentine's Day 1938. But a more likely explanation rests with the manufacturer's postal address; Vickers-Armstrong Ltd, Engineers, Newcastle Upon Tyne. Between 1940 and 1944 8,275 Valentines were built in eleven different marks, 1,420 of which were produced in Canada (of which all but 30 were shipped to the Soviet Union).

Unlike the Matilda and several other British designs, the Valentine's turret ring was large enough to allow the tank to be up-gunned although it was a tight squeeze in the turret and the commander had to act as a loader (**right**). So Mk I to VII Valentines were armed with a 2pdr gun, Mks VIII to X with a 6pdr gun and the Mk XI with a

75mm gun. Valentines were fitted with several different engines during their production life. Mk Is were powered by an AEC petrol engine, Mk IIs and IIIs with an AEC diesel engine (**left**), and later models were fitted with six-cylinder GM two-stroke liquid cooled diesels. The Valentine weighed around 17 tons and its armour varied between 8mm and 65mm thick. It had a fairly respectable maximum speed, for an infantry tank, of 15mph reducing to about 8mph cross-country. It is said to have been reliable and generally liked by its crews despite having a poor driving position (**below**) and heavy controls. Valentines saw most of their action in the Western Desert.

The spotless Valentine Mk II illustrated (**bottom left**) is the product of seven months of solid restoration work and is pictured fresh from the Kent workshops of UK armour collectors Rex and Rod Cadman. The bare hull was discovered rusting away in deepest Cornwall without interior, top-decking, stowage boxes or skirts, all of which had to be either located or fabricated. The turret was found on a firing range in Wales. The engine that came with the hull was found to be beyond saving, but luckily another similar engine was sourced from an enthusiast in Yorkshire who specialised in all things AEC and from the two engines a completely original Valentine engine was reconstructed. The gearbox and rear-drive are all original but rebuilt, about which Rod Cadman comments, 'typically British, everything totally over-engineered and far more complicated than it ever needed to be'.

A range of special-purpose derivatives was based on the Valentine chassis including a bridgelayer, the Scorpion mine clearance vehicle and one of the most successful self-propelled guns of the war, the Archer. There was also a duplex-drive amphibious Valentine developed and used for pre-D-Day training.

Infantry Tank Mk IV Churchill

The A22 Infantry Tank Mk IV, or Churchill as it became known, was yet another product of outmoded thinking among Britain's General Staff; heavily armoured, slow and under-gunned. Not a bad tank, you understand, but a tank in the wrong war at the wrong time and frequently at a disadvantage in combat against more agile, better armed German designs. With the expectation that the Second World War would be fought along the same trench-bound lines as the First World War, the General Staff issued in September 1939 a specification for a new Heavy Infantry Tank, the A20. The specification called for a heavily armoured vehicle with a maximum speed of 9mph able to cross a 16ft trench and a 7ft vertical obstacle. It was to be armed with a field gun in the front hull plus a pair of 2pdr guns in side sponsons and two machine-guns. The crew were to number eight. In essence the specification outlined a mildly updated First World War tank.

When two mild steel pilot models emerged in June 1940, overweight and under-powered, the project was cancelled. In its place the Department of Tank Design issued a more modern specification to Vauxhall Motors asking them to design a tank powered by their new 350hp Bedford Twin-Six engine. It was essential that at least 500 of the new tank be produced by mid-1941 so Vauxhall pulled out all the stops to produce a mock-up by November 1940, commence testing of the prototype the following month, complete the first production model in March 1941 and make first deliveries to the Army on 30 June of the same year.

As is almost inevitable when a vehicle is rushed into production the Churchill experienced a host of minor problems throughout its first year in service. The tank's baptism of fire was the abortive raid on Dieppe in August 1942. The Churchills were unable to cope with Dieppe's steep shingle beach and all were either knocked out or captured, so presenting the Germans with intact examples of Britain's latest tank. Half a dozen

Churchills shipped to North Africa to take part in the second battle of El Alamein in October 1942 fared better. Despite what the Dieppe débâcle may have indicated, Churchills had an excellent cross-country performance and their armour, up to 152mm thick, made them all but immune to contemporary anti-tank fire. They were generally popular with their crews.

Eleven basic marks of Churchill were produced all weighing around 40 tons and having a crew of five; driver, assistant driver, gunner, loader and commander. Top speed was generally around 13mph and operational range about 120 miles. Mk Is were armed with a 2pdr gun in the turret and a 3in howitzer in the front hull, but the Mk II deleted the howitzer in favour of a 7.92mm Besa machine-gun. Mk IIIs and IVs were up-gunned to 6pdrs in new turrets – welded and cast respectively. In addition, from the Mk III onwards the top runs of the Churchill's tracks were enclosed. Later marks incorporated minor improvements to the drivetrain and increased armour protec-

tion and were armed with either a 75mm gun or 95mm howitzer. Unfortunately even the 75mm gun was unable to make much impression on German heavy armour and the Churchill's hull and turret ring were too narrow to allow further up-gunning.

Several special-purpose Churchills were produced including an armoured recovery vehicle, bridge layer and a flame-thrower known as 'Crocodile'. A few late model Churchills saw action in Korea, but the type was shortly thereafter retired from service. Few Churchills survive in working order. The vehicle illustrated (**above**, courtesy of Mark Ansell), a Mk VII 'Crocodile' flame-thrower, was restored at great expense and no little difficulty by the Budge Collection.

Cruiser Tank Mk VIII (A27L) Centaur

The A27L Centaur was the more successful of two interim models between the Cruiser Mk VI Crusader and the Cruiser Mk VIII Cromwell. Around 950 were produced from late 1942. The original plan had been to power the Centaur with the V-12 600bhp

Rolls-Royce Meteor engine later fitted to the Cromwell. However, the RAF had prior call on that engine (which was essentially a modified Merlin as used by Spitfires) and the Centaur was instead fitted with the same engine that powered the Crusader, a 395bhp Liberty Mk V V12. It was coupled to a new five-speed Merrit-Brown gearbox and controlled differential and gave the Centaur a top speed of 24mph.

Most of the 6pdr gun armed Centaurs were used for training, but 90 Centaur Mk IVs, the close-support version armed with a 95mm howitzer, were shipped to Normandy in 1944 and used by the Royal Marine Armoured Support Regiment. The tank illustrated (**below**) was one of that batch and is preserved by the Caen Canal at Pegasus Bridge in Normandy, site of the daring first British airborne landings on D-Day. The tank came ashore at Sword Beach on D-Day with part of V Troop of the 5th Independent Battery of the RMASR. About 500 yards inland it was set ablaze by mortar fire and abandoned. After the war the hulk was bought by a scrap dealer. In 1975 it was recovered and, after restoration by REME engineers, put on display at its present site in June 1977.

There were at least six special-purpose Centaur variants produced, notably two mounting twin Polsten guns for anti-aircraft use. Otherwise most Centaurs were converted into Cromwells in 1943 by the retro-fitting of the Rolls-Royce Meteor engine.

Cromwell Mk VIII (A27M)

British General Staff policy during the 1930s led to there being two basic categories of tank in service during the Second World War; infantry and cruiser. The former were ponderous and heavily armoured as befits a tank intended for infantry support. The latter were fast but relatively lightly armoured and looked upon as the mechanised equivalent of cavalry, putting speed before firepower and protection to exploit potential breakthroughs on the battlefield. However, combat experience with the pre-war designed Covenanter and Crusader cruisers revealed that both were under-armed and under-armoured. So in 1941 a specification was issued calling for a heavy cruiser with armour between 65mm and 75mm thick and able to mount a 6pdr gun. Of the designs that emerged the Cromwell was by far the most successful. Production started in January 1943 by which time it was realised that tanks exploiting breakthrough situations usually found themselves facing infantry and soft targets rather than other tanks. It was therefore decided to fit some later production Cromwells with a 75mm dual-purpose gun similar to that used by Shermans and able to fire both armour piercing and high-explosive shells.

There were eight different marks of Cromwell produced. Apart from the armament there was little to tell them apart externally. Cromwell Mks I, II and III were armed with 6pdr main guns, Mks IV, V and VII with a 75mm main gun and Mks VI and VIII with a 95mm howitzer. All weighed about 28 tons, were powered by a 600hp V12 Rolls-Royce Meteor engine and were capable of almost 40mph. Steering was effected by a Merrit-Brown gearbox which controlled the transmission of power from the engine to one or both tracks. Pulling back on one steering lever caused the selection of a differential steering gear and slowed the track on the same side while speeding up the other. The lower the gear selected the tighter the turn. Track brakes were mounted separately and operated simultaneously by the main brake pedal.

Cromwells first went into action with the 7th Armoured Division, the famous 'Desert Rats', when they landed in Normandy on D-Day+1 in June 1944. Combat in Normandy's bocage country, a patchwork of small farms, woods and lanes separated by high-banked hedgerows, favoured the defensive deployment of German heavy armour and disadvantaged the nimble Cromwell. Outmatched in firepower and armour, the Cromwell was only able to show its true worth after the breakout from Normandy when it was able to exploit its manoeuvrability and speed. Although Shermans provided the bulk of medium tank strength within British armoured units, Cromwells were comparable and saw a considerable amount of action. If the Cromwell had one major shortcoming it was that its narrow turret was unable to accommodate a 17pdr gun, the sole British anti-tank weapon able to engage heavy German tanks at long range.

The A27 Cromwell pictured (**above**, courtesy of Mark Ansell) was recovered from the firing ranges on Salisbury Plain and completely restored to running condition by the Budge Collection.

A34 Comet

The A34 Comet (**right**) was a development of the Cromwell armed with a short-barrelled 76.2mm Ordnance Quick Firing Gun said to be about the equal of the 17pdr fitted to the Sherman Firefly. It also had an all-welded hull and turret with armour up to 101mm thick and improved Christie-type suspension. The Comet had a five-man crew: commander, driver, gunner, loader and assistant driver who also operated one of the two Besa machine-guns.

The engine was the same V12 Rolls-Royce Meteor as used in the Cromwell driving via a five-speed Merrit-Brown gearbox with controlled differential. Since the Comet was heavier than the Cromwell its maximum top speed was less at around 29mph and the radius of action about 120 miles. The Comet entered service at the end of 1944 and at last gave the British Army a tank that could engage all but the heaviest of German armour on something

approaching equal terms. It was probably the best British tank design to see action in the Second World War and remained in service with the British Army until 1960. This nice example (**previous page and above**) is part of the Imperial War Museum's collection at Duxford.

Centurion

The Centurion is arguably Britain's most successful tank to date. Between 1945 and 1961 a total of 4,423 were manufactured by the Royal Ordnance Factory, Vickers, and Leyland Motors. The design dates back to 1943 when the Directorate for Tank Design commenced work on a heavy cruiser tank under the designation A41 with the intention that it should be able to engage Germany's fearsome new Tiger tank on equal terms. High speed was not necessarily important but armour protection and firepower were. By May 1944 a mock-up had been produced which mounted a 17pdr multi-purpose gun. The chassis featured a sloping glacis plate and a modified Horstmann suspension instead of the Christie type previously

favoured. Twenty pilot models were ordered, fifteen armed with the 17pdr gun and five armed with the same 76.2mm gun fitted to the Comet.

In May 1945 the first six A41 prototypes were shipped out to the 22nd Armoured Brigade in Germany to see how they would perform under active service conditions. Unfortunately they did not arrive until after the cessation of hostilities, but nevertheless the new tank was well received by serving crews. By that time development was already underway on the A41A with thicker armour, a cast – as opposed to fabricated – turret, coaxially mounted Besa machine-gun and other improvements. 100 A41s and 100 A41As (Centurion Mk 1 and 2 respectively) were ordered. Most Mk 2s were later brought up to Mk 3 status by up-gunning with a 20pdr.

From 1957 onwards Centurions were fitted with a 105mm gun and an improved fire control system, a modification which was estimated to give the updated tank a 25% better chance of scoring a hit. From the Mk 5 onwards, in addition to the main gun, Centu-

rions were fitted with a coaxial .30 calibre Browning with another mounted on the commander's cupola. Centurions carried a crew of four: the driver in the front right hand side of the hull and the other three crew members in the turret; commander and gunner on the right and loader/radio operator on the left. The hull was of all welded steel construction and the turret was cast with the top plate welded in. Armour thickness varied from 17mm to 152mm. There were eventually no less than 25 different marks of Centurion gun tank all being powered by the highly reliable Rolls-Royce Meteor 12-cylinder 600hp engine, a development of the famous Merlin aero engine. Most marks had a top speed of 20mph and an operational range of about 120 miles, neither figure being particularly outstanding.

About half of the Centurions manufactured were exported to, among others, Denmark, the Netherlands, Switzerland, Sweden, India, Jordan, South Africa, Kuwait and Israel. It was Israel that solved the speed and range problem by retro-fitting its Centurion fleet with American 750hp Continental diesel engines. This modification immediately increased the Centurion's top speed by 50% and its operational range by almost 100%. South Africa followed a similar course showing that one reason for the Centurion's longevity was its development potential. Centurions may have arrived too late to see action in the Second World War, but they did not have to wait long to prove themselves in combat. Mk 3s served with distinction in Korea and were judged by many to be the best tank of the war, far superior to the Soviet designed T-34/85. When in action with the Indian Army in 1965, Centurions were said to have proved superior to Pakistan's US-designed M47s and M48s and in Israeli hands proved absolutely lethal when up against Egypt's Soviet supplied armour.

The Chieftain MBT started to replace the Centurion gun tank in British Army service from 1967 although special-purpose variants continued in service for much longer. Quite a few Centurions are in private and museum collections. The two examples illustrated (**right and below**) are based at Duxford.

Centurion ARV

Several specialised Centurion variants were produced including an Armoured Bridge-layer and, illustrated here (**above**) by another vehicle from the Imperial War Museum collection, the FV4006 Centurion Armoured Recovery Vehicle (ARV) Mk 2. They were produced by the Royal Ordnance Factory, Leeds and entered service with Royal Electrical and Mechanical Engineer (REME) units of the British Army in 1956. It is based on the Centurion Mk 3 chassis with the turret replaced by a fixed superstructure. The vehicle is equipped with a winch capable of towing a load up to 31,000kg plus a 10-ton capacity lifting jib. There is a large earth anchor at the rear. Armament was restricted to a single .30 machine-gun.

Centurion AVRE

Yet another variant of the reliable Centurion, and an unusual choice for the private collector, is the Armoured Vehicle Royal Engineers (AVRE). This is a direct descend-

ant of 'Hobart's Funnies', the range of specialised vehicles operated by General Hobart's 79th Armoured Division throughout 1944–5, and was developed for demolition, clearance and gapping duties. The first prototype appeared in 1957 and most of the production vehicles were manufactured at the Royal Ordnance Factory in Leeds during the early 1960s. The FV4003 Centurion Mk 5 AVRE 165, as it is properly designated, was based on the Centurion Mk 5 with a 165mm demolition gun, or 'bunkerbuster', replacing the original 20pdr gun. The 165mm gun fires a HESH (High Explosive Squash Head) projectile powerful enough to destroy large structures and is accurate up to a range of about 2,200 yards. At the hull front is a hydraulically operated dozer blade with a fascine cradle above. The 'skull and crossbones' flying from this vehicle (**left and above**) mark it as one of a veritable fleet of armour owned and maintained by members of the Duxford Aviation Society's Vehicle Wing.

FV432 Armoured Personnel Carrier

The FV432 was in its day by far the most numerous of all the tracked vehicles used by the British Army. The prototype appeared in 1961 and was in production with GKN Sankey from 1962 until 1971. There are four basic marks of FV432; the Mk 1 had its exhaust system prominently mounted on the left hand side of the hull, whereas the Mk 1/1, Mk 2 and Mk 2/2 all had their exhausts routed over the vehicle's roof. The FV432's hull is basically a steel-plate box varying between 6mm and 12mm thick and is large enough to accommodate up to ten infantrymen plus driver and commander. The main access doors are at the rear but the driver and commander each have their own hatches and there is a further four-piece circular hatch over the main compartment. The 240hp Rolls-Royce K6000 No. 4 Mk 4F engine is mounted at the front and gives the FV432 a maximum road speed in the region of 32mph.

When closed down only the driver and commander have external vision devices and there is no way for the embarked infantrymen to use their personal weapons unless a hatch is opened. Some FV432s have a dismountable 7.62mm machine-gun by the commander's hatch, but the vehicle resplendent in the Berlin style urban camouflage scheme (**see overleaf, top**) is fitted with what is known as a GPMG turret in place of the main roof hatch. This manually operated turret mounts a 7.62mm L37A1 machine-gun. Integral wading screens give FV432s a reasonable amphibious performance with propulsion from the tracks. The list of variants is lengthy and includes a command vehicle, ambulance, cargo carrier, mortar carrier and so on.

Surplus FV432s can be bought for a few thousand pounds and, as they are relatively easy to drive (**see overleaf, centre**), are a popular choice for the military vehicle collector who wants to gain experience of

tracked vehicles. Two tillers, one for each track, take care of steering and braking. Pulling back on a tiller brakes the track on that side and causes the vehicle to turn in the chosen direction. Hauling back on both tillers brings the vehicle to a stop. Gears are selected via a stubby short-throw shift lever on the driver's left and, being semi-automatic, there is no clutch pedal to be concerned about. A very user friendly vehicle.

FV434 Maintenance Vehicle

The FV434 was specially developed from the FV432 for use by Royal Electrical and Mechanical Engineer units. It has an open topped cargo compartment and is fitted with a hydraulic HIAB crane with a two-piece jib capable of lifting AFV engines and other heavy items. Another feature of the FV434 is its ability to lock the torsion bars on its front and rear axles for additional stability while the crane is in use. The usual crew consists of a commander, driver/crane operator and two fitters. A canvas tilt can be erected to protect the open rear compartment from the elements and there is also provision for the fitment of a 7.62mm L7A2 or L7A4 machine-gun. The privately owned example illustrated (**bottom left**) fulfils exactly the purpose for which it was designed, i.e., assists in the maintenance of a private collection of tanks. No Chieftain owner should be without one!

Tracked Rapier

The Tracked Rapier was originally developed by British Aerospace and mounts a Rapier surface-to-air missile launcher on a chassis related to that used by the American M113 armoured personnel carrier built by FMC. The Imperial Iranian Armed Forces ordered a batch, but the order was cancelled when the Shah of Iran was overthrown and BAe were left with a number of vehicles, a large development bill and no customer. However, the British Army showed an interest and in June 1981 placed an order for 50 which was subsequently increased to 70. First examples were delivered to the British Army of the Rhine in January 1984.

The Tracked Rapier's eight missiles are contained in an armoured launcher which can be manually loaded in about five minutes. The vehicle's crew of three are accommodated in a cramped forward cab protected by 25mm thick aluminium armour. The 240hp GMC Model 6v-5T diesel engine sits directly behind the crew compartment and, unfortunately for maintenance personnel, is said to take 29 hours to change as the cab and most of its contents need to be removed in the process. Two other problems encountered when the Tracked Rapier first went into service were short track life and the auxiliary power unit (an APU powered the vehicle's complicated systems when in action) having a 'dirty' exhaust which made the vehicle all too easy to spot. That this Tracked Rapier (**above**) was snapped up by an enthusiast when the demise of the British Army of the Rhine led to vehicles being made surplus only goes to prove that there is a market for even the most esoteric vehicle.

Conqueror

The Conqueror (**right**) was developed to meet the threat of the Soviet IS-3 heavy tank which first appeared in 1945 and boasted a

122mm gun and armour up to 160mm thick. Conqueror, designated FV214, was powered by a water-cooled Rolls-Royce M120 V12 fuel injected engine capable of producing 810hp at 2,800rpm. Despite having such a powerful engine, armour between 1in and 3in thick and a combat weight of 65 tons means that this massive beast can barely attain 20mph and has an operating range of only about 95 miles. The sloped and well rounded cast turret mounts a 120mm gun which owes its origins to an American designed anti-tank gun. The ammunition is unusual in that a large brass shell case holds the propellant and is separate from the projectile. Rounds were therefore large and heavy and only 35 could be stowed at any one time.

The first pilot model emerged in 1952 and by 1955 twenty were undergoing trials with the British Army of the Rhine. Only 180 Conquerors were produced and its relatively short service life, from 1955 to 1966, perhaps reflects the many mechanical and electrical faults which plagued the design and its alleged general unpopularity with crews. Nevertheless, as 'last of the heavies' in British Army service it is an impressive beast worthy of note. One of about a dozen examples preserved, this Conqueror (**previous spread and top left**) belongs to the Imperial War Museum .

Conqueror ARV

A massive tank requires a massive recovery vehicle and 'Persuader' fits the bill perfectly. Based on the Conqueror chassis but with a fixed superstructure and equipped with the usual complement of heavy duty winch and dozer blade, this beast (**opposite page, bottom**) has more than enough muscle power to extract the heaviest vehicle from the mire.

Chieftain

'So where do you park it?'
'Anywhere I like!'
The old jokes are the best, and watching 55 tons of FV4201 Chieftain tank grind a Datsun Sunny into oblivion (**below**) certainly appealed to the spectators' collective sense of humour at a recent show organised by the Invicta Military Vehicle Preservation Society.

Until the arrival of the Centurion in 1945 British tanks had either been under-gunned, under-armoured or both. A specification issued in 1958 by the General Staff for a tank to replace the Centurion recognised that unfortunate fact and called for an agile, thickly armoured tank armed with a weapon capable of engaging enemy AFVs at long range. Leyland were selected as design leaders and their L60 multi-fuel engine as the new tank's powerplant. With hindsight an unfortunate choice.

The first Chieftain prototype emerged in 1959 and six more were delivered by 1962. Trials revealed a host of problems with the gearbox, suspension and, in particular, the engine. The multi-fuel concept was an interesting one, but a nightmare to engineer, and early engines were unable to deliver the 700bhp required. By the time engine power had been raised to the specified level Chief-

tain was overweight, which meant the suspension had to be strengthened which added even more weight. As a result Chieftain is neither as fast nor as manoeuvrable as had originally been hoped.

Although Chieftain was accepted for army use and first examples were issued in May 1963, a succession of teething problems led to protracted trials and development work and meant that it did not finally enter service as the British Army's first Main Battle Tank (MBT) until 1967. Arguably Chieftain's best feature was its 120mm L11A5 gun which, when coupled to an excellent fire control system, gave the tank a lethally accurate punch. In terms of firepower and protection Chieftain was a match for any of its

contemporaries although it lacked the speed and manoeuvrability of French and German MBTs.

Chieftain's hull is of welded construction with the exception of the front which is cast, as is the turret. The driver sits centrally and low down to keep the hull height to a minimum and when his hatch is closed adopts an almost fully reclined position using a periscope for vision. The commander and gunner occupy the right-hand side of the turret with the loader on the left. In addition to the excellent 120mm gun, which can fire a variety of ammunition including HESH (High-Explosive Squash Head) and APDS (Armour Piercing Discarding Sabot), there is a 7.62mm machine-gun fitted coaxially and provision

for another to be mounted on the commander's cupola.

Between 700 and 800 Chieftains were built for the British Army in over a dozen different marks each incorporating various improvements. Unfortunately the Chieftain's Achilles' heel remained its Leyland L60 engine and transmission which never lived up to expectations despite undergoing modification while in service. Now replaced by Challenger, there are a surprisingly large number of Chieftains in private hands (**right**) despite the problems associated with maintaining such a large and complex vehicle. In fact several enterprising companies in the UK have purchased surplus Chieftains and offer all-comers the opportunity to experience the thrill of driving a main

battle tank (**left**). Whatever mechanical problems Chieftain may have experienced in service, it does make for an excellent big boy's (and girl's) toy. Large, imposing and noisy, yet simple enough for a complete beginner to drive – albeit under close supervision. Left- and right-hand tillers control the tracks, a foot pedal on the left shifts the gears (press down to change down, lift up to change up) and a foot pedal on the right controls the throttle. All you need is a large empty space, lots of practice and your own gas station!

Chieftain ARV

When Chieftain was introduced it was decided to develop a compatible armoured recovery vehicle to replace the Centurion Mk 2 ARV. Design work started in 1964 and the first prototypes appeared in 1971. Full production of the FV4204 ARV commenced at Vickers' Works, Newcastle upon Tyne, in 1974, but it was not until 1976 that vehicles were accepted for service and issued to REME (Royal Electrical and Mechanical

Engineers) units. The Chieftain ARV is based on the Chieftain Mk 5 to which numerous changes have been made. To accommodate the main winch the driver's position has been moved to the left with the commander's hatch, complete with 360 degree revolving cupola, directly behind. Within the main compartment there is room for a further two or three crew members.

Mounted on the front is a dozer blade on hydraulic rams primarily intended to be used to stabilise the vehicle when the winches are in use although it can be used for clearance purposes. Two winches are fitted, both driven by power take-off from the main engine. The main winch has a 30,000kg capacity (increased to 90,000kg with the dozer blade dug-in) and the secondary winch has a 3,000kg capacity.

The vehicle illustrated (**left, top and bottom**) is actually a Chieftain Armoured Repair and Recovery Vehicle (ARRV Mk 2). When the Challenger MBT entered service existing FV434 REME repair vehicles were unable to handle the weight of its engine. So, as an interim measure until a Challenger ARRV could be put into service, Chieftain ARVs were converted to ARRVs by mounting an Atlas hydraulic crane on the left-hand side and a heavy duty engine stand at the rear.

Abbot

During the Second World War the advantages of self-propelled artillery were readily apparent and the British Army fielded a variety of SP guns including the Sexton (a 25pdr gun on a Ram chassis) and Priest (105mm on a Sherman chassis). The FV433 Abbot (**below**) continued the line of warlike clerics and is based upon the ubiquitous FV432 chassis. The first prototype was

completed in 1961 and the Abbot entered service in 1964. It has a crew of four with the driver seated at the front of the hull (**left**) and the other three crew members seated in the turret at the rear. The Abbot mounts a 105mm L13A1 gun with a manual elevation of –5 to +70 degrees and a full 360 degree power traverse. It is powered by a 240bhp Rolls-Royce K.60 Mk 4G engine and is capable of 30mph.

With the withdrawal of the British Army of the Rhine (BAOR) and a general slimming down of resources, many Abbots have been declared surplus and have been purchased by collectors for the price of a second-hand family saloon (**opposite page**). Spares are relatively easy to obtain and there is plenty of ex-army expertise around to help with maintenance.

Scorpion

The Scorpion CVRT (Combat Vehicle Reconnaissance Tracked) (**below**) was designed to fulfil a need for an economically priced air-portable armoured vehicle to replace the wheeled Saladin and Saracen and equip mobile strategic forces. Alvis Ltd of Coventry won the design contract in 1967, the first prototype was completed in 1969

and, in 1970, the go-ahead was given for a family of vehicles based on the same basic components. The Scorpion's hull and turret are made from an aluminium-zinc-magnesium alloy and it is powered by a militarised version of Jaguar's XK J60 4.2 litre six-cylinder engine similar to that fitted to their sports saloons.

Scorpion's alloy armour only effectively protects the three-man crew from small-calibre fire, but contributes greatly to the vehicle's overall light weight (the tracks are said to exert less pressure than a walking man). One Scorpion can be carried in a sling beneath a Chinook helicopter or two

loaded into a C-130 Hercules transport plane. The lightweight construction also means that the Scorpion is capable of an astonishing maximum theoretical road speed of well over 60 mph – forwards or backwards! Cross-country performance is also excellent as was proved when, during the 1982 Falklands War, the Blues and Royals operated four Scorpions and four Scimitars to good effect. Armament consists of a 76mm main gun with a 7.62 mm coaxial machine-gun.

The Scorpion is very popular with AFV collectors (**below**): fast, reliable, easy to maintain and enormous fun to drive – even on public roads! But you'd be lucky to get much more than four miles per gallon.

USA AND CANADA

M3A1 Scout Car

The White M3A1 was essentially the first purpose-built four-wheel-drive scout vehicle used by the US Army. The open topped hull was constructed of ¼in armour plate with ½in thick hinged plates over the windscreen and side door windows. In addition to a driver and commander, six infantrymen could be carried. The four-ton M3A1 was powered by a six-cylinder JXD Hercules engine (**right**) – the same engine that powered the Studebaker US6 6x6 truck – and was capable of a maximum speed in excess of 55mph.

Variants included a diesel engined version designated M3A1E1, the M3A1E2 with an armoured roof, the M3A1E3 which mounted a 37mm gun behind the cab area and M3A1 Command Car which had higher armoured sides and an armoured windscreen. Almost 21,000 M3 series Scout Cars

were built between 1940 and 1944, with more than half going to Allied forces as the US Army considered the vehicle outmoded and unable to match half-tracks in any respect. After the war large numbers of vehicles were donated to European Governments under the Marshall Plan which aimed to assist shattered European armies to re-equip by supplying surplus US Army vehicles. The Greek Army received around 1,000 M3A1s and have recently sold off a surplus batch. About 50 came to the UK and many have been purchased by private collectors and restored. Unfortunately for them, under the terms of the original Military Assistance Programme Greece had to 'fully demilitarise and render unserviceable to prevent use by hostile nations' all vehicles before passing them to their new owners. In other

words take a cutting torch to the vehicles and reduce them to armour plate jigsaws. So as well as locating hard to find parts, the new owners have had to painstakingly match and weld back together dozens of pieces.

Looking at the pristine ex-Greek Army M3A1s pictured (**previous spread and top left**) it is hard to believe that they were not so long ago little more than piles of scrap. According to the proud owner of 'Deadly Di' the importing dealer undertook most of the basic heavy tasks, but it has taken him over two years of painstaking detail work to get the machine into good-as-new prize-winning condition. Note the armament of one .50 calibre mounted behind the cab and a pair of .30 calibre machine-guns mounted on a skate rail at the rear. As is

often the case with these heavy utilitarian vehicles it is hard work to drive and prone to overheating if left idling too long. White Scout Cars preserved in desert markings are few and far between. This vehicle (**bottom left**) once served with the French Foreign Legion and now bears the markings of the 7th Armoured Division 'Desert Rats'.

GMC Otter Mk I Light Reconnaissance Car

The Otter Mk I (**below**) was General Motors of Canada's version of the Humber Mk III Light Reconnaissance Car. It utilised the same chassis as their C15TA armoured truck and was powered by a six-cylinder 106hp GM 270 engine driving the rear or all four wheels via a four-speed gearbox and single-speed transfer box. The welded hull

was constructed by the Hamilton Bridge Company from armour plate varying in thickness from 8mm to 12mm. It was armed with a Boys anti-tank rifle firing through a port to the driver's left and a single Bren gun mounted in the open-topped turret. 1,762 were built in 1942 with most being used by Canadian units in Italy, although it was used in smaller numbers by the British Army and RAF Regiment.

The vehicle illustrated (**above and previous page**) was discovered derelict on an Essex farm in 1982 lacking the screen, rear body, roof and turret. During the eighteen months it took to restore the vehicle inside (**left**) and out, a turret was found in Alberta, Canada, and other missing parts either sourced or remade. It bears the markings of the Headquarters Company, 7th

Armoured Division serving in Tunisia circa 1943. Since restoration this Otter, believed to be the only running example in private hands, has proved remarkably trouble free transporting its owner to vehicle rallies as far afield as Normandy.

Mk I Fox Armoured Car

The Fox Mk I was General Motors of Canada's version of the Humber Mk III Armoured Car. It was powered by a rear-mounted GMC 270 engine and armed with .30 and .50 calibre Browning machine-guns. The welded hull and turret were manufactured by the Hamilton Bridge Company. Only some 1,500 Fox series vehicles were produced in 1942/43 so there are few still in existence. The Fox illustrated (**above**) is finished in late-war 'Mickey Mouse ears'

camouflage and marked up as a 7th Armoured Division vehicle.

M8 Armoured Car

Just as the Germans' successful usage of armoured cars during the opening stages of the Second World War had prompted the British to develop their own range of wheeled armoured vehicles, so it persuaded the US Army that it too needed a light, fast armoured car for reconnaissance duties. They chose the T22, a vehicle armed with a 37mm gun which had originally been developed by the Ford Motor Co. as a tank-destroyer. By that stage of the war it was realised that a 37mm gun would barely dent a German tank's armour so the vehicle was given a new purpose in life by simply reclassifying

it as the M8 Light Armoured Car. It was put into production in March 1943 and by the time the assembly lines closed in 1945 8,523 had been manufactured.

The M8 is powered by a rear-mounted six-cylinder 79hp Hercules engine driving either all six or just the rear wheels via a four-speed Hydramatic transmission and two-speed transfer box. Spreading the vehicle's eight-ton weight over six large wheels gave it a relatively low ground pressure and makes for an excellent cross-country performance for this type of vehicle. The M8's 56mph maximum speed caused it to be nicknamed the 'Greyhound' in British service. It carried a crew of four: driver and assistant driver in the front hull, and commander and gunner in the turret. In addition to the M8's 37mm main gun there

was a coaxially mounted .30 calibre machine-gun. A later version, the M8E1, also had a .50 calibre anti-aircraft machine-gun on a ring mount.

By the end of the war the US Army had lost its enthusiasm for the M8 having found it under-armoured and under-gunned and were starting to phase them out. The Korean War extended the M8's service life briefly, but thereafter remaining vehicles were made surplus or passed over to the National Guard. Allied and Third World armies continued to use the M8 for many years and that is probably why there are still so many in existence. The M8 illustrated (**above**) is owned by a French collector and was photographed while waiting to take part in a parade to commemorate the 50th anniversary of the liberation of Bayeux. The other vehicle (**left**), an M8E1 complete with .50 calibre ring mount, is ex-Italian Army, owned by a Belgian and photographed in England. The

mudguards have been removed for ease of driving on public roads as have those on the M20 finished in Free French markings (**above**). This vehicle was recovered in very poor condition from a firing range and still bears the scars of many hits.

M20 Armoured Utility Car

The M20 is simply a turretless version of the M8 armed with a single .50 calibre machine-gun on a ring mount. It entered production in March 1943 and the Ford Motor Co. built 3,791 before the lines closed in 1945. The M20 was used as a scout car, command vehicle and even as a cargo carrier. It could seat four passengers in addition to its two-man crew. The drivetrain and running gear were identical to the M8's and the vehicle is just as popular among AFV collectors. Spare parts are relatively plentiful and inexpensive and there are reported to be some 70 to 80 M8s and M20s in private hands (**right**).

Staghound

During the Second World War British industrial capacity was stretched to breaking
point and clearly unable to meet the
demands imposed upon it. Therefore Great
Britain relied greatly upon American and
Canadian production facilities for all
manner of military hardware. One case in
point is the Staghound Armoured Car. It was
a joint British/American design originally
intended for use in North Africa. Unfortunately, or fortunately depending upon your
point of view, fighting in North Africa had
ceased by the time Chevrolet started
making deliveries and the Staghound only
saw combat in Western Europe.

Larger than most contemporary
armoured cars, the Staghound is an
imposing 18ft long and 8ft wide, and had a
crew of five. Twin GMC six-cylinder 97bhp
engines drive all four wheels via a Hydramatic transmission and propel the 14-ton
beast to a maximum speed of 55mph. The

operational range was about 450 miles.
Staghound's cast turret mounted a 37mm
gun with coaxial .30 calibre machine-gun. A
second .30 calibre machine-gun was fitted
in the hull front and late production models
had additional twin .30 calibre guns
mounted on the turret roof for anti-aircraft
protection.

Close to 3,900 were built between 1942
and 1944 with the vast majority being used
by British Commonwealth armies. After the
war many served on with European NATO
armies, in particular Belgium, the Netherlands and Denmark. Only a very few have
since found their way into private collections. Before being sold off as surplus this
rare example (**above**) had been severely
cut up as required under the terms of the
original military aid programme. The
restorers in the UK did a fine job of putting
it back together again and it now resides in
an American collection. Similar magic will
shortly be worked upon the Staghound

bearing the badge of the 2nd Polish Corps
which, when photographed (**top right**), still
awaited the installation of its restored
engine and transmission.

International and White Half-Tracks

During the Second World War half-track
vehicles were extensively used by both
Allied and German forces. In the late 1930s
the US Army developed a particular enthusiasm for the concept and sponsored a
'marriage' between the wheeled M3A1
armoured scout car and soft-skin M2 half-
track truck. The prototype T7 appeared in
1939 and subsequently became the Car,
Half-Track, M2, a ten-seater armoured
personnel carrier. That same year specifica-
tions were laid down for a similar scout car
which resulted in the T14 prototype. Even
as testing continued the Ordnance Department upped its half-track requirement
vastly and the T14 was standardised as the
Carrier, Personnel, Half-Track, M3 (**right**).

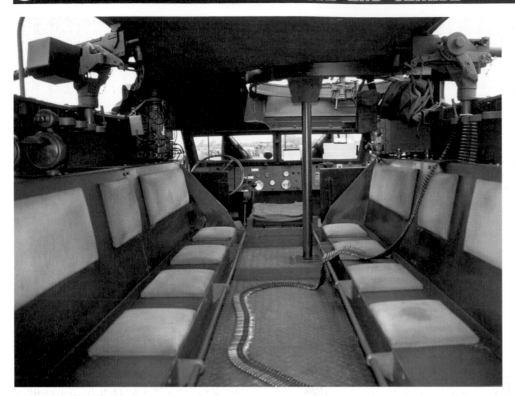

Harvester Corporation joined in the manufacture of half-tracks from 1942. Their versions of the M2 and M3, designated M9 (**below**) and M5 (**right**) respectively, were similar in most respects to those produced by the three other companies. The most obvious differences were that International's half-tracks were powered by their own Red Diamond RED 450B engine, the bodies had rounded rear corners and the front mudguards were of a flat section.

Armour protection was limited to $\frac{1}{4}$in except for the windscreen and side door shields which were $\frac{1}{2}$in thick so was only effective against small-calibre fire. Fitted with either White's or International's engine most models had a top speed in excess of 45mph. Front wheel drive capability and reinforced rubber tracks on a vertical volute suspension system gave the series a good off-road ride and capability. The spring-loaded drum frequently mounted on the vehicle's front bumper (**bottom right**) was intended to stop it digging in when negotiating ditches or steep banks. Including prototypes there were over 70 different variants produced on the basic theme ranging from the standard .30 and/or .50 calibre

It was slightly longer than the M2 and had a 13-man capacity (**above**).

To standardise production of the two vehicles an engineering board was set up composed of representatives from the Ordnance Department and each of the three chosen manufacturing companies: White, Autocar and Diamond. Among the components adopted as standard were White's 160AX engine and the Spicer four-speed transmission. To increase production and meet the needs of Lend-Lease, International

armed M3 and M5 to the T12 gun motor carriage mounting a 75mm artillery piece. Other variants mounted mortars, anti-aircraft guns and howitzers, and there was the usual range of ambulance, command car, radar and wireless vehicles. The total production of half-tracks between 1941 and 1945 exceeded 40,000 and at the end of the war thousands were left in Europe surplus to requirements and subsequently handed over to, in particular, France, Belgium, the Netherlands and West Germany. A large number also ended up with the Israeli Army who later re-engined them with diesel engines and used them well into the 1980s.

This restored White M16 (**above**) is fitted with a fully operational (but non-firing) quad .50 calibre anti-aircraft gun turret and is ex-French Army stock. It passed through the hands of various dealers before being acquired by the present owners in a very sorry condition. Three years of work later it is almost as good as new. The chevrons on the doors were copied from a Second World War training film and are recognition marks applied so that company commanders could identify their own unit's vehicles.

T16 Universal Carrier

The T16 (**right**) was the US designed and built equivalent of the British Universal Carrier and was manufactured solely at the Ford Motor Company plant in Somerville, Massachusetts, from March 1943. Ford engineers incorporated many improvements in their design. For increased strength and ease of manufacture the T16's hull was of welded not riveted construction. It was larger than the Universal Carrier and powered by a 100hp V8 Ford Mercury engine mounted centrally and driving the rear sprockets via a four-speed gearbox and controlled differential. The T16 was right-hand drive and was steered via two levers in front of the driver. The Horstmann type suspension was similar to that used by the British Universal Carrier but had four bogie wheels rather than three. By the time the production line closed in May 1945 13,893

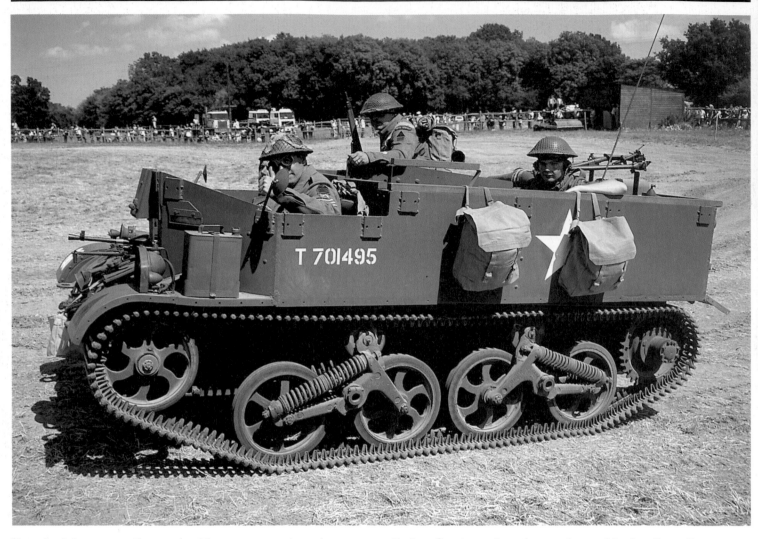

T16s had been manufactured with most going to British and Canadian forces.

Illustrated (**previous page and above**) is a 1944-built T16 which was bought by a scrap dealer after the war to use as a run-around in his yard. It was rescued by a military vehicle enthusiast and slowly restored over many years. It is crewed by battle re-enactors dressed as soldiers serving with the 1st Battalion, Royal Norfolk Regiment. They are part of a group who support the Royal Norfolks' museum and various veteran and charitable organisations.

M3A3 Stuart

'It's a horrendous thing to drive,' says the co-owner of this 1943-built M3A3 Stuart, the only operational example of its type in the UK (**right and opposite page, top**). 'Everything about it is brutal. The clutch is fierce and it's very hard to steer. It usually needs two hands to do anything. Even

starting the seven-cylinder Continental radial engine from cold is hard work. The engine must first be manually rotated with

32 turns of a cranking handle to disperse any oil which may have seeped past the piston rings into the lower cylinders.' A comment at

odds with the fact that early production M3s shipped out to North Africa in 1941 were dubbed 'Honeys' by their British crews because, so the story goes, they were considered 'a honey of a tank'. Obviously expectations were lower in those days.

Some 14,000 M3 light tanks were produced in five basic marks differentiated by a combination of welded, riveted or cast-welded turrets and riveted or welded armour plate hulls. The M3A3 (Stuart V in British service) entered production in 1943 and was the final model. It had an all welded hull, weighed about 16 tons and was capable of 36mph with a range of 80 miles. M3s were fast and reliable, but hopelessly outgunned and were declared obsolete by the US Army in 1943, although they served with Allied armies throughout and well beyond the Second World War.

This particular tank once served with the British Army and is painted to represent a vehicle attached to the 7th Armoured Division in the European theatre during 1944–5. The serial number actually represents the date the owners finished the first stage of restora-tion. The interior (**below**) has been cleaned up and stripped of all non-essentials but was clearly a cramped place to fight a war.

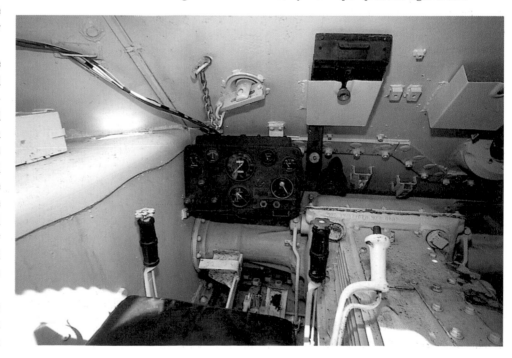

M5A1 Stuart

The Continental radial engine that powered most of the M3 series of light tanks was originally an aero engine and became more difficult to obtain as aircraft production increased. Therefore Cadillac were charged with producing a prototype for an M3 replacement powered by two Cadillac V8 auto engines coupled to a pair of their newly developed automatic Hydramatic transmissions. In the event so many changes were made to the basic M3 that the resulting tank was designated as a new model, the M5.

It first went into production at Cadillac's Detroit factory in March 1942 and was gradually phased in to replace M3 production at other factories. Early in 1943 the M5A1 was introduced featuring a modified turret, larger driver's and co-driver's hatches and numerous other improvements. M5s were marginally smaller than M3s but had thicker armour – between 12mm and 67mm – and a slightly greater range. Although the top speed remained the same 36mph, M5s were much easier to drive, quieter and very reliable. The turret featured a power traverse system and, although the M5 was armed with the same 37mm main gun as the M3, it was gyrostabilised for better accuracy while firing on the move. Nevertheless, and despite thicker armour and improved fire control, M5s were still at a distinct disadvantage when up against German tanks and anti-tank weapons and were declared obsolete by the US Army in 1944.

Some 8,884 M5 and M5A1 tanks were produced, 1,400 of which were used by the British Army and known as Stuart VIs. After the war large numbers of surplus M5s were passed on to other countries with whom they served for many years. In fact several Third World countries used them until quite recently. The M5 is a far more pleasant driving experience than the M3 and, because of its size, light weight and use of automotive parts in its drivetrain, is a popular choice for the private collector. (**below and right**).

M3 General Lee

When war broke out in Europe in 1939 America was the only major nation that had no tank force to speak of. Nor did it have the means to manufacture tanks in any quantity. No doubt prompted by events on the other side of the Atlantic, General A. R. Chaffee was put in charge of the newly created Armored Force in July 1940 and lost no time in meeting with the Ordnance Department to discuss future tank requirements. It was

superstructure. It weighed a little under 28 tons and was originally designed to accommodate a crew of seven: commander, driver, two gunners, two loaders and a radio operator. The 75mm gun was mounted in a sponson on the right-hand side of the hull and a turret with a 37mm gun was fitted offset to the left. Both guns had gyrostabilisers. M3 design work finished in March 1941 and by August of that year full-scale production was underway at the purpose-built Detroit Arsenal. Orders were also placed with the American Locomotive Co. and the Baldwin Locomotive Works, and almost 6,000 M3 series medium tanks were built before production ceased in December 1942.

US Army M3s first saw action in Tunisia following the Operation 'Torch' landings in November 1942. They suffered serious losses partly because of the US crews' lack of battle experience. M3s also served with the Australian Army and this example (**below**, courtesy of Bob Fleming) was recovered from Western Australia for the Budge Collection.

decided that a new medium tank be designed incorporating a 75mm gun and heavier armour than the existing M2A1. Unfortunately the means of mounting such a large gun in a 360 degree revolving turret did not exist at the time, so as a stop-gap measure,

and in the interests of getting a tank with adequate firepower into production, it was proposed that the new tank mount the gun with limited traverse within its hull.

The new design utilised the M2A1's chassis and running gear, but with a new

There were six basic models:

M3 Powered by a Wright nine-cylinder air-cooled radial engine and with a riveted hull with side doors. This was the most numerous model with almost 5,000 being produced.

M3A1 Cast hull.

M3A2 All welded hull (only a dozen built).

M3A3 All welded hull and powered by twin six-cylinder GM Series 71 diesels.

M3A4 Riveted hull lengthened to accommodate a Chrysler 30-cylinder multibank engine.

M3A5 Riveted hull and powered by twin GM diesels.

M3 General Grant

In American service the M3 medium tank was known as the General Lee. The British Army, having lost most of their tanks during the evacuation from Dunkirk, were grateful recipients of around 700 of a modified version which they dubbed the General Grant. The most obvious difference between the Lee and the Grant was that the latter's turret was made slightly larger to accommodate a radio (and so reduce the crew to six) and of a lower silhouette since it lacked the Lee's large cupola with integral machine-gun. Grants were shipped to North Africa in 1942 and performed well against Rommel's Afrika Korps when they went into action for the first time at the Battle of Gazala on 27 May 1942. At last the British Army had a tank capable of engaging German Panzer IIIs and IVs from beyond the effective range of the German guns.

This fine example (**below**, courtesy of Bob Fleming), another Budge Collection vehicle, is known to have been used to train American troops at a desert training centre in California before being shipped to British forces in India. It went on to fight against the Japanese in Burma and was then shipped to Australia. In the 1950s the Australian Army sold it as surplus and it was discovered on a farm being used as a bulldozer prior to being shipped to the UK in 1988 for a ground-up restoration.

M4 Sherman

It was recognised by the US Army as early as 1940 that to counter the threat posed by German AFVs any future medium tanks should have heavier armour protection and, at the very least, a 75mm main gun. The first

tank to result from this decision was the M3 which, because there was little experience of mounting a gun of such weight and calibre in a revolving turret, had a 75mm gun mounted in a sponson on the front right-hand corner of the hull. M3s performed well, but were seriously disadvantaged in combat by the fact that the 75mm main gun had a very limited traverse which frequently meant that the whole tank had to be turned to bring the gun to bear.

As soon as design work on the M3 finished early in 1941 attention had turned towards developing its successor, the M4, and by May of that year a mock-up had been produced. After minor modifications the T6 prototype was demonstrated at Aberdeen Proving Grounds in September. It was armed with a 75mm gun in a 360 degree revolving turret mounted on a one-piece cast hull and had the engine and chassis of an M3. The crew numbered five: commander, gunner and loader/radio operator in the turret, driver and assistant driver/bow machine-gunner in the hull. Production was immediately authorised. Eleven plants including those of Chrysler, Ford and General Motors went on to manufacture almost 50,000 M4 Sherman series tanks between 1942 and 1945. It was not the best tank of the Second World War, but it was certainly the most numerous.

The M4 Sherman series was originally intended to be powered by a modified aero engine, the Wright Continental R-975 radial. However, since there were not enough of these engines available to meet demand, the M4 design was modified to accommodate several other engines. To detail fully M4 production would take an entire book, but essentially there were six basic models:

M4 The original design with a welded plate hull and powered by a Wright Continental R-975. Early versions had a three-piece bolted nose later replaced by a combination cast and rolled nose.

M4A1 Mechanically the same as the M4, but with a cast one-piece hull as typified by 'Combat Camel' which belongs to the Brussels Tank Museum (**above right and right**).

M4A2 Similar to the M4, but powered by two coupled General Motors 6-71 diesel

engines. Shown here is 'Calvados' from the Tank Museum's collection (**above and opposite page**). It has the late model HVSS suspension and a 76mm gun.

M4A3 Similar to the M4, but powered by a Ford GAA V8 petrol engine. Had a one-piece cast nose.

M4A4 The rear hull was lengthened to accommodate a Chrysler multibank tank engine consisting of five six-cylinder car engines joined. Had a three-piece bolted nose.

M4A6 Similar to the M4A4, but powered by an Ordnance RD-1820 air cooled diesel and having a sharply profiled cast and rolled nose.

(The missing M4A5 designation was allotted to the Canadian Ram II.)

During the production life of the M4 four types of main gun were used: 75mm, 76mm, 105mm and 17pdr, with the result that there were several sub-model designations relating to armament. The adoption of the horizontal volute suspension system (HVSS)

led to even more sub-model designations, but a comprehensive list is beyond the scope of this book.

In time the US Ordnance Board carried out comparative trials on all the different engines and established a preference for the Ford GAA V8 so the M4A3 became the most numerous of the variants and was kept almost exclusively for US Army use. Runner-up was the Wright R-975 followed by the GM diesel and the difficult to maintain Chrysler multibank. In the interests of

rationalisation the Ordnance RD-1820 was never a contender, and only 75 M4A6 variants were produced.

Although the M4 series corrected many of the M3's shortcomings it was still under-armoured and possessed a relatively high profile. Nothing could be done about the latter without seriously interrupting production, but extra armour plate was frequently welded on to Shermans in service and crews tended to attach spare track links, bogie wheels and even sandbags to vulnerable areas for a little extra protection. Wet ammunition stowage was also introduced after combat experience showed that direct hits on the Sherman's side – where the ammunition was stowed – frequently led to combustion. In fact the Germans nick-named Shermans 'Tommy Cookers' because of their propensity to catch fire. The ammunition stowage area was redesigned to incorporate ethylene glycol or water filled jacketing which, when pierced, flooded the stowage area and greatly reduced the likelihood of combus-

tion. An improvement negated when crews took to carrying extra unstowed ammunition in their vehicles.

The Sherman's original 75mm gun proved incapable of dealing with heavily armoured German tanks and, from March 1944, a 76mm gun in a larger turret with a distinctive bulge to the rear was introduced. Superior though the new gun was, it was still unable to penetrate a Tiger's or a Panther's 100mm frontal armour. Although a new high-velocity shot was developed for the 76mm gun, which proved quite effective it was only when the British installed a 17pdr anti-tank gun in the Sherman turret and created the Firefly that Sherman crews were able to take on the German big cats from a reasonable range with any real chance of success.

As the M4 Sherman evolved so it became heavier. A larger turret and 76mm gun plus other improvements such as wet ammunition stowage increased the Sherman's weight to nearly 35 tons. The M4's original track and vertical volute

suspension had come in for criticism because of its poor ride quality and short spring life – a situation only made worse as the tank's weight increased. In 1941 Chrysler had developed a horizontal volute suspension system (HVSS) for a heavy tank project which never reached fruition. However, HVSS was adapted and tested on M4s together with a wider track (23in across compared with the original 16in track) and the combination was adopted as standard on all M4s produced after August 1944. The resulting 'E8' designation led to them being nick-named 'Easy Eights'. With the new suspension and 76mm gun the Sherman had reached the zenith of its wartime development. It was still behind the Panther and Tiger in terms of firepower and armour protection, but was faster, more manoeuvrable and, perhaps more important, had an overwhelming superiority of numbers.

Late model Shermans went on to serve in Korea, but retired from US Army service in 1956. Several other countries held on to

their Shermans for many years, notably the Israelis who up-gunned and up-engined their fleet and retained their so called 'Super Shermans' until the 1970s. They are now appearing in private collections such as this fine example owned by US collector Jacques Littlefield (**above**, courtesy of Hans Halberstadt). The M4A1E8 'Easy Eight' illustrated (**below**), gained a certain notoriety when it narrowly avoided being impounded and its crew arrested by Normandy police after it was alleged to have chewed up several kilometres of road during the 50th Anniversary of D-Day celebrations in 1994. It wouldn't have happened 50 years previously! Shermans of any variety are not particularly pleasant to drive. The controls are not hydraulically

assisted and radial engined models are not as tractable as other variants and are therefore prone to stalling when manoeuvring at slow speed.

The Sherman was adapted for just about every purpose you could imagine: mine flail, recovery vehicle, plough, earth mover, assault bridge, flame-thrower, rocket launcher ... the list goes on. The M4 was nothing if not adaptable.

Grizzly

To augment US production, Canada built a version of the M4A1 Sherman at the Tank Arsenal, Montreal Locomotive Works, mostly using components shipped in direct from the United States. Known as the Grizzly, only 188 were produced in late 1943 before it was realised that US production could cope with demand. The Grizzly is easily recognisable from its cast hull, emblazoned on the front with a large 'G' (**upper left**). As Grizzlys are fitted with Wright Continental R975 radials, before starting from cold a crew member must manually turn over the engine via a cranking handle to disperse oil which may have gathered in the lower cylinders. The Portuguese Army sold off a couple of dozen Grizzlys to a UK dealer in the early 1980s. Except that their gun barrels had been cut off many were in reasonable condition and form the bulk of the UK's Grizzly population. The driver of this example (**left**) demonstrates the fine art of negotiating a 'knife edge'.

M7 Self-propelled Artillery Vehicle (Priest)

In 1941 it was decided to develop a self-propelled artillery gun capable of keeping up with fast-moving armoured formations. The resulting M7 was introduced in April 1942 and was simply the standard US Army 105mm field howitzer mounted in an open-topped slab-sided superstructure on the chassis of an M3 medium tank. The pulpit-like .50 calibre anti-aircraft machine-gun mount on the hull's right front led to the M7 being known as 'Priest' in British Army service.

Almost 4,000 M7s were produced based on the M3 medium tank chassis, with a

further 826 being based on the M4A3 Sherman chassis and designated the M7B1. They remained in service with the US Army until after the Korean War and large numbers were passed on to other countries under military aid programmes. This particular vehicle (**above and left**), originally part of the Budge Collection, was recently offered for sale by a UK dealer for around £30,000.

Sexton Self-propelled Gun

The British Army were so impressed with the Priest that they decided to copy the concept and produce their own version. They had the Tank Arsenal, Montreal Locomotive Works, mount the British Army's standard 25pdr gun on the chassis of the Ram tank (itself based on the US M3 design). Unlike the M7's 105mm howitzer, the 25pdr had a double-baffle muzzle brake and was capable of both direct and indirect fire. It was even used successfully as an anti-tank weapon on occasions. Like all Canadian vehicles built for British service it is right-hand drive.

Between 1943 and 1945 2,150 Sextons were built and they served with the British Army until the 1950s. Sextons were also employed by the Indian, South African and Portuguese Armies and most of the vehicles still in existence are from ex-Portuguese stock. Both the fully restored 'Boadicea' and 'Beau Brummel' (**above and right**) bear the twin 'Ts' (for Tyne Tees) of the 50th (Northumbrian) Infantry Division.

M10 Tank Destroyer

In 1941 the US Army created the Tank Destroyer Branch. Having noted that static anti-tank defences had proved unequal to the task in Poland and France, their intention was to attach battalion sized mobile anti-tank units to army divisions tasked with opposing mass tank attacks anywhere on the battlefield, or destroying enemy tanks so that friendly armour could effect a breakthrough. Initially anti-tank guns were mounted on trucks or half-tracks, but in 1942 the Tank Destroyer Branch received

their first purpose-built fully tracked tank destroyer, the M10.

The M10 mounted a 3in gun in an open-topped five-sided turret on the chassis of a Sherman M4A2 or, as the M10A1, on a Sherman M4A3 chassis. The 3in gun had originally been designed as an anti-aircraft weapon and when fitted to the M10 had its 42in recoil shortened to about 19in. Apparently this modification caused the vehicle to rock viciously each time the gun was fired and some crews took to attaching ballast weights to the M10's turret for extra stability. Over 6,000 were built in total and they saw action in Tunisia, Europe and the Pacific. The M10 carried a five-man crew and, because it was lighter than the heavily armoured Sherman, was capable of almost 30 mph. The British Army up-gunned many of the 1,700 they had by installing a 17pdr as fitted to the Firefly. The result was known as the Achilles.

Since the M10 shares many components with the ubiquitous M4 Sherman some parts are relatively easy to source. Nevertheless, restored M10s remain comparatively rare. The M10A1 pictured at a vehicle rally in the UK (**below**) has since crossed the Atlantic to a US collection.

M24 Chaffee

The US Army were not slow in recognising that its M3 and M5 series of light tanks were inferior to contemporary German designs, certainly in terms of firepower and protection. So to redress the balance Cadillac started work on a prototype known as the T24 in 1943. Like the M5 before it, the new tank was powered by a pair of V8 water-cooled Cadillac car engines, but linked to a manual two-speed and reverse gearbox rather than an automatic transmission. The pilot T24 was completed in October 1943 and judged so successful that an order was

immediately placed. Production M24s (later named Chaffees in honour of General Adna A. Chaffee) started rolling off the production line in April 1944. Only limited numbers were shipped to Europe, but they saw action during the Battle of the Bulge, the crossing of the Rhine and during the final advance into Germany.

The Chaffee was armed with a new light-weight 75mm gun which had originally been developed to fit into a version of the B-25 Mitchell medium bomber. The gun utilised the same ammunition as the M4 Sherman's gun, but with its short barrel and lower muzzle velocity was not so effective against heavy armour. The Chaffee's own armour was no more than 1 inch thick. In addition to the 75mm main gun, Chaffees were armed with a .30 calibre machine-gun mounted coaxially, another in a ball-mount on the hull front, and a .50 calibre machine-gun mounted on the turret roof.

Chaffees again saw combat action in Korea in 1950 when, as the only United Nations' tanks in position, they faced a North Korean advance spearheaded by the formidable T-34/85. It was not an even match and they struggled until relieved by heavier Sherman, Centurion and Patton tanks. The Chaffee was an excellent tank for its intended purpose and, although replaced in US Army service by the M41 in the mid-fifties, appeared in the inventories of almost two dozen Allied armies. Like the preceding M5, the M24 is a popular collectors' item. It has more interior space, no turret basket, a relatively smooth ride thanks to the torsion bar suspension system, and is easier to drive than its predecessors (**right**).

M40 Self-propelled Gun

The success of the M7 led to there being a demand for more self-propelled artillery and in March 1944 work began on a pilot vehicle designated T83 able to mount a newly developed 155mm gun. The Sherman M4A3E8 chassis with horizontal volute spring suspension was chosen as the basis for the new SP gun although it had to be widened and strengthened. Standardised as the M40,

it went into production early in 1945 at the Pressed Steel Factory, Pittsburgh, and around 300 were manufactured before the war ended. There was also an unarmed cargo carrying version to transport additional gun crew and ammunition. This M40

(**below**) is maintained in working order at the Imperial War Museum, Duxford.

LVT(A)4 Alligator

Shown making its debut appearance after restoration is this rare LVT(A)4 Alligator

amphibian (**above and below**). Around 18,000 LVTs (Landing Vehicle Tracked) were manufactured between 1941 and 1945 of which some 3,118 were LVTAs (Armoured). The 75mm howitzer armed LVT(A)4 and 37mm gun armed LVT(A)1 were designed to reduce casualties during assault landings by accompanying unamoured troop-carrying variants such as the LVT4 Water Buffalo. An improved version of the LVT(A)4 with a power turret traverse and designated LVT(A)5 was introduced in 1945 too late to see action. The LVT(A)2 was a cargo carrying version of the LVT(A)1 armed only with one .50 and one .30 calibre machine-gun.

The deeply cleated 14-inch-wide tracks are driven by a Continental W670-9A radial

engine and would no doubt have given the pristine Alligator illustrated a reasonable amphibious performance. However, they did not appear to cope particularly well with the parched grass on which it was displayed.

M26 Pershing

Well before D-Day the US Army had been debating the issue of a replacement for the Sherman without ever reaching any firm conclusion. The most promising result of development work was the T26E1 which mounted a new 90mm gun. However, there was some disagreement as to how many were needed and whether in fact a 76mm gun would be preferable, and it wasn't until January 1945 that a small batch was shipped to Europe. The new tank performed well and in March 1945 it was standardised as the heavy tank M26 Pershing (after General Jack Pershing) and put into full production. Only about 300 Pershings were shipped to Europe before the war ended and, of those, it is said that only 20 saw action. However, they were to play a major part in the Korean War.

The 41-ton M26 was powered by a 500hp Ford GAF petrol engine which drove the rear sprockets via a Torqmatic transmission and gave the Pershing a maximum speed of 30mph and a range of about 100 miles. The hull and turret were of cast construction and much better armoured than the Sherman's. It had a five-man crew and, in addition to the 90mm main gun, carried two .30 calibre machine-guns – one coaxially and one bow-mounted – and a .50 calibre machine-gun mounted on the commander's cupola.

It is thought that there are only three or four Pershings restored to running order. The example shown (**above**, courtesy of Frank Buck) is an early production model aptly named 'Amago Del Diablo' (Friend of the Devil) and is one of the star attractions of a prominent US collection.

M41 Walker Bulldog Light Tank

The M41 was intended to replace the M24 Chaffee as a light reconnaissance tank. When authorised for production in 1949 the M41 was to be called the Little Bulldog, but was later re-christened the Walker Bulldog in honour of General Walton W. Walker who was killed in an accident during the Korean War. The first production models were completed in Cadillac's Cleveland Tank Plant in 1951, but entered service too late to see action in Korea. Like the Chaffee, speed and manoeuvrability were of the essence, so the M41's armour was relatively thin – between $1/3$ and $1^1/2$in thick. Most M41s were powered by a Lycoming or Continental six-cylinder 500hp engine, but late production M41A3s were fitted with an uprated fuel injected version which marginally increased the tank's original 100 miles operating range. Whichever engine was fitted resulted in a top speed of around 45mph .

The Walker Bulldog's hull is of all welded steel construction and the turret is of welded and cast construction. It carried a crew of four in a cramped interior. The driver was particularly unlucky in that the turret overhung his position and while he had his head out of the hatch he must have lived in constant fear that the turret would be unexpectedly traversed. Other than that and the fact that the engine and transmission were considered to be extremely noisy, crews are said to have generally appreciated the Walker Bulldog for its reliability and good handling characteristics. The M41's main armament consisted of a 76mm

gun the barrel of which was fitted with a bore evacuator and 'T'-type blast deflector. In addition, a .30 calibre machine-gun was mounted coaxially and a .50 calibre Browning machine-gun was attached to the commander's cupola. (**above and right**)

Some 5,500 Walker Bulldogs were built between 1951 and 1959 and, although it was replaced in US Army service by the M551 Sheridan in the late sixties, it served on for a good many years with those two dozen or so armies to whom it had been exported. Several hundred went to the South Vietnamese Army who had a notable success with them in March 1971 when a detachment clashed with NVA armour in Laos and destroyed six T-54 and sixteen PT-76 tanks for no loss.

M44 Self-propelled Howitzer

Development of the M44 dates back to 1947 when work started on a 155mm self-propelled howitzer designated T99. Having decided to utilise various components of a

new light tank, the T41, which was later to become the M41 Walker Bulldog, the project was re-designated T99E1 and 250 vehicles were built. An upgraded version, the T194, was put into production and then standardised in 1953 as the M44. All 250 T99E1s were subsequently brought up to M44 specification. Early model M44s are powered by an air-cooled Continental AOS-895-3 six-cylinder petrol engine, but the M44A1 introduced in 1956 has a fuel injection system fitted. Maximum road speed is 35mph with a range of about 75 miles.

The M44's hull is of all welded construction to a maximum armour thickness of $\frac{1}{2}$in. The fighting compartment at the rear has no overhead protection other than steel hoops over which a tarpaulin can be fitted (**above**). The standard 105mm howitzer is capable of firing high-explosive, chemical, nuclear, smoke and illuminating rounds, and around 24 projectiles can be carried internally. For self-protection a .50 calibre machine-gun can

be mounted at the left-hand corner of the fighting compartment.

M47 Patton

By the time the Korean War broke out in 1950 the US Army's standard medium tanks were the M26 Pershing and the M46, an upgraded M26 with a new transmission and engine. There was a new medium tank, the T42, being developed, but it was not yet ready for production. So in order to meet the pressing need for an improved medium tank the T42's turret was grafted onto the M46's hull and chassis and the result became the M47. Production got underway at the Detroit Tank Arsenal and the American Locomotive Company in June 1951 and 8,576 M47s were produced between then and November 1953.

The all cast construction M47 weighed 55 tons and its armour varied between $\frac{1}{2}$ and $4\frac{1}{2}$in thick. Main armament was the M36 90mm gun with a .30 cal machine-gun mounted coaxially. The M47 also had a .30

calibre mounted in the glacis plate and was the last American tank to have a bow-mounted machine-gun. Power was supplied by a Continental AV-1790-5B 12-cylinder air-cooled engine mated to a CD-85 cross-drive transmission. Maximum road speed was 30mph and it had a range of about 80 miles.

Despite being rushed into production the few that were shipped to Korea didn't see combat. In fact the M47 was plagued with problems, particularly with the fire control, and did not last long in US Army service before being replaced by the M48. Large numbers of M47s were passed on to NATO and other armies and it first saw action in 1956 in the hands of the French during the Suez Campaign. In 1965 Pakistani M47s were in action against their Indian neighbours and in 1967 Jordanian M47s fought with Israeli Shermans. Spanish M47s also saw plenty of action playing the role of King Tigers in one of the armour enthusiast's all-time favourite films, 'Battle of the Bulge'.

There are a number of M47s in private hands despite their size and weight, although the vehicle illustrated (**above**, courtesy of Fraser Gray) is displayed at the Panzermuseum, Thun. Engine spares are reasonably priced and the engines are said to be fairly easy to maintain. One big advantage of the type is that it has dual controls so the owner can safely give or receive driving lessons.

M48 Patton

The M47 had been rushed into production and numerous problems surfaced as soon as it entered service. In October 1950, well aware of the M47's shortcomings, the US Army prompted the Detroit Arsenal to produce a design study for a new medium tank. It was to have improved armour protection, lower ground pressure, longer range and a more efficient fire control system – all while retaining the good manoeuvrability of the M47. Two months later the design study was approved and Chrysler awarded a contract to complete design work and build six prototypes desig-

nated 'Tank, 90mm gun, T48'. The first prototype was completed in December 1951, production commenced in 1952, and first deliveries were made to the US Army in 1953.

The M48 Patton's hull and turret are of cast armour construction, 120mm at their thickest points. The hull front has a distinctive boat-like 'bow' to help deflect mine blast, and the design took account of the possibility that a larger turret/gun combination might be fitted at a later date. The engine and transmission were the same as fitted to the M47, but since the M48 was heavier and carried less fuel its battle range was reduced to about 75 miles and it had a maximum road speed of 30mph. The M48A3 introduced in the late fifties was powered by a 750hp V12 diesel engine which greatly improved the tank's operational range.

The M48 was the first American tank to have a single driver. He is seated at the front centre of the hull while the gunner, loader and commander occupy the turret. The main armament is a 90mm M41 gun. In addition, either a .30 calibre or 7.62mm

machine-gun was mounted coaxially to the main gun and a .50 calibre machine-gun incorporated in the commander's cupola (with the exception of the M48A1 which carried a .50 calibre machine-gun on a conventional mount). After the Vietnam War many M48A3s were up-gunned with a 105mm gun and re-designated M48A5.

The rugged strength of the M48 series was best illustrated on 3 May 1955 when, during Exercise Desert Rock VI, three unmanned M48s were placed only 500 yards from the detonation of a 35–40 kiloton atomic weapon. Although damaged they survived the blast and were driven away! The M48 first saw real combat in 1965 with the Pakistani Army during border clashes with India. It did not fare well against the Indian Army's Centurion and Sherman tanks, but in truth the lack of success was more likely a reflection of the Pakistani crews' inability to operate the M48's relatively sophisticated systems rather than any fault in the tanks themselves. The M48 got its first blooding with the US Army at Ben Het on 3 March 1969 in the only direct

American tank versus NVA tank battle of the Vietnam War. During the night action a platoon of Pattons destroyed two NVA PT-76s and a BTR-50 armoured personnel carrier at no loss to themselves. Later clashes between Vietnamese Republican M48s and NVA PT-76s and T-54s were similarly conclusive.

Some 12,000 M48 tanks were produced before the lines closed in 1959. Having been relegated to Reserve and National Guard units they were phased out of US service in the late eighties, but still continue in service among more cost-conscious armies. A handful of M48s are in private hands. The M48A3 illustrated (**above and right**, courtesy of Hans Halberstadt) was originally supplied to the Jordanian Army as an M48. It was captured by the Israelis who converted it to M48A3 status by replacing the engine and transmission. The well travelled tank changed hands again when it was captured by the Egyptian Army after having being knocked out by an RPG during the Yom Kippur War of 1973. It was purchased and restored to working condition by the

now defunct Budge Collection and currently resides in the United States.

M103 Heavy Tank

The M103 was America's answer to the IS range of Soviet heavy tanks which entered service just as Cold War paranoia was escalating. It is basically a lengthened M48 hull on to which has been mounted a massive turret mounting a 120mm gun. Some 300 were produced by the Chrysler Corporation in the early fifties but teething problems delayed their entry into service with the US Army and Marine Corps until 1956. They did not have a long service life (neither, in fact, did the IS-3 or the Conqueror, Britain's equivalent). Advances in weapons technology produced guns of equal power to the 120mm, but compact enough to be fitted into smaller tanks. In other words the differences between medium and heavy tanks eroded to a point where one category of tank would suffice – the main battle tank – and the M103 became obsolete.

The M103 was originally powered by a Continental petrol engine which gave it a top speed of 21mph, a range of about 80 miles and consumed fuel at the rate of three gallons per mile! The M103 faded from US Army service during the early sixties, but the Marine Corps held on to theirs a decade longer during which time they received an upgraded fire control system and were re-engined with Continental diesels – a modification which increased the tank's range to around 300 miles. As such they were designated M103A3. Owing to their size and weight, and the fact that so few were built in the first place, there are very few M103s still running. This ex-Marine Corps tank (**top left and left**) has recently been acquired by the Tank Museum, Bovington, and is seen here being put through its paces at their annual 'Battle Day' in 1997.

M75 Armoured Personnel Carrier

The M75 (**below**) was the US Army's first fully tracked armoured personnel carrier with overhead armour protection. It was designed to carry a standard ten-man infantry squad plus a driver and commander and was ordered into production in 1952. Between then and 1954 1,729 were built by FMC Corporation and International Harvester Co. It was powered by a 295hp six-cylinder Continental engine and had a maximum speed of about 40 mph. The box-like hull was constructed of armour plate between 1/4in and 1in thick, but the engine air-cooling grilles on the side were considered a potential weakness.

The 18-ton M75 wasn't amphibious and even as it was entering service the US Army was planning to replace it with FMC's smaller, fully amphibious M59 APC. As the M59 started to enter service so the M75 was phased out. Many were passed on to the Belgian Army under a military assistance programme and used by them until the early eighties. The programme required that the vehicles be returned to the US Government when they were no longer

required and most were thereafter sold for scrap. However, at least two dozen are thought to have ended up in private collections. The M75 may not have been particularly successful, but it set the trend for future APC development.

M113 Armoured Personnel Carrier

Since 1959 around 90,000 M113 and M113A1 Armoured Personnel Carriers have been produced by FMC Corporation in the United States and OTO-Melara in Italy, a staggering number, particularly when coupled with the knowledge that the M113 is, or has been, in service with no less than 50 countries in addition to the United States. A fact which must make it the most widely used armoured vehicle of all time. The M113 originated from a US Army requirement, drawn up in 1954, for a family of airportable tracked vehicles to replace the M59 and M75 APCs

then in service. Prototypes were ready by 1958 and production started in 1959. The first production run of M113s were powered by a 209hp Chrysler petrol engine, but from 1963 onwards a 275hp GMC 6V53T diesel engine was substituted and the vehicle was re-designated M113A1. Top speed with either engine is around 40mph, but the diesel makes for a superior operational range of about 300 miles as opposed to the 100-mile range offered by the petrol engine.

A combat ready M113 (**above**) only weighs about eleven tons largely because of its novel construction of welded aluminium armour. On the down-side, the 1in thick plate only protects against small arms-fire, shell fragments and the like. Typically the vehicle is configured to carry eleven infantryman plus a commander and driver and is armed with a single .50 calibre machine-gun mounted on the hull roof. A

large hydraulically operated ramp at the rear allows for easy access. There is a small door within the ramp for use when necessary and a large roof hatch through which the passengers can also enter or exit.

M113s first saw action in 1961 with the South Vietnamese Army who fitted them with extra guns and used them almost as if they were tanks, an ill-advised policy in that a standard M113 offered little if any protection against large calibre weapons and no protection at all for the poor exposed gunner. The South Vietnamese therefore fitted many of their vehicles with locally developed gun-shields. When the US Army arrived in large numbers in the late sixties it was decided that similarly modified M113s would replace tanks in cavalry platoons. So they followed the South Vietnamese example and fitted an armour shield to the .50 calibre machine-gun and added

pedestals and shields for two further M60 machine-guns. The result was known as the ACAV (Armoured Cavalry Assault Vehicle). As might be expected a large number of special-purpose variants were developed based on the basic M113 chassis, including a command and control vehicle, a mortar carrier, several missile carriers, an anti-aircraft gun carrier and a flame-thrower.

M60 MBT

In the mid fifties work started on a replacement for the M48 Patton. Prototypes of what was to become the M60 appeared in 1958 and were basically modified, re-engined and up-gunned M48s. The gun chosen for the new tank was the British-designed 105mm L7 which, when slightly modified and manufactured in America, became the M68. A production order was placed with Chrysler and the M60 went into production at the

Detroit Tank Arsenal late in 1959 with first deliveries being made to the US Army in 1960. These early production M60s still looked very much like M48s except that they had a flat glacis plate, a larger commander's cupola and fewer track return rollers. In 1962 the improved M60A1 (**above**, courtesy of Hans Halberstadt). entered production with, among other things, a larger, redesigned turret with a better ballistic shape. The 58-ton M60A1 is of all-cast construction with armour up to 120mm thick. The driver is seated at the front centre of the hull and the other three crew members occupy the turret. The M60 is powered by a 750bhp Continental AVDS-1790-2a 12-cylinder diesel engine and is capable of 30mph on good going with a range of around 310 miles.

The M60A2, which commenced development in the mid-60s, but which did not enter

service until 1974, featured a new turret fitted with a 152mm gun/launcher capable of firing either conventional ammunition or the Shillelagh missile. About 500 of this version were manufactured, but it was not particularly successful and only served with the US Army. In 1978 a major upgrade to the M60A1's systems, including a new fire control and engine, led to the re-designation M60A3. M60s served with the US Marine Corps during Operation 'Desert Storm', but have now all but disappeared from service with US Forces. They have also seen combat with the Israeli and Iranian Armies and were exported to Saudi Arabia, South Korea, Turkey, Egypt, Thailand, Italy and Austria among others.

About 15,000 M60s were produced which is not bad for a tank originally introduced as a stop-gap measure when the M48 appeared to be outgunned by the Soviets' T-54/55 series.

The US Army are not selling their surplus M60s to collectors, but are said to be willing to swap them for any particularly rare vehicles sought by an Army museum. Shown is one of the very few M60A1s in private hands (**top left**, courtesy of Hans Halberstadt). Certainly they are more likely to be seen in museum collections such as this M60A3

being displayed with great gusto at the Imperial War Museum's incomparable annual military vehicle show – a must for any armour enthusiast (**left and above**).

M551 Sheridan Light Tank

Very rare in private hands, and illustrated here with an example owned by American

super-collector Jacques Littlefield, (**overleaf**, courtesy of Hans Halberstadt) is the M551 Sheridan. It was in service with the 82nd Division, the last unit to use the type, until 1996. The Sheridan came out of a requirement issued in August 1959 for a 'new vehicle with increased capabilities over any other weapon in its own inventory and that of any adversary'. The Allison Division of General Motors took up the challenge to meet the requirement by designing a vehicle known as the Armoured Reconnaissance Airborne Assault Vehicle (ARAAV). The first prototype emerged in 1962 and the first production M551 Sheridans rolled off the line in 1966. Around 1,700 were produced before production ceased in 1970.

The Sheridan's hull is of aluminium construction and its turret is of welded steel. Probably its most unusual feature is the 152mm gun/missile launcher which can fire both conventional ammunition and the Shillelagh missile which is guided to its target by a two-way infra-red command link. In theory the tank's gunner simply has to keep his sight crosshairs on the target and a hit is assured. Eight missiles can be carried together with 20 rounds of ammunition. The Sheridan also carried a 7.62mm machine-gun coaxially and a shielded .50 Browning on the commander's cupola.

RUSSIA

BRDM-2 Reconnaissance Vehicle

The BRDM-2 entered service with the Soviet Army in the early sixties and has been exported to almost 40 sympathetic countries. It was a development of the open-turreted BRDM-1 which was equally widely exported. The BRDM-2 is amphibious, being propelled by a single water jet at the rear. Between the front and rear axles are a pair of retractable, chain driven wheels (**right**) which can be raised and lowered by the driver to aid cross-country performance. The seven-ton vehicle usually has a four-man crew and is powered by a GAZ 41 V8 petrol engine. Top speed is said to be in the order of 60mph with an operating radius of 400 miles.

The small turret, the same as that used on the BTR-60 APC, is fitted with one 14.5mm and one 7.62mm machine-gun and is remotely and manually operated. There were several variants of the basic BRDM-2 including a range of missile launchers. This vehicle (**below**) is ex-East German Army.

BTR-60 APC

The BTR-60 armoured personnel carrier entered service in the 1960s and is closely related to the smaller BRDM-2 reconnaissance vehicle. It has the same 14.5mm and 7.62mm machine-gun armed turret and is also amphibious. In addition to a crew of two, fourteen infantrymen can be accommodated in the vehicle's boat-like hull. It is fully amphibious, being propelled in the

water by a single hydro-jet at the rear (**top left**). Twin GAZ-49B engines power all eight wheels. The BTR-60 illustrated (**bottom left**) is also ex-East German Army stock now preserved in working order by the Imperial War Museum.

KV-1 & KV-2

In 1938 the Soviets commenced the design of a heavy tank that was to be almost impervious to 37mm anti-tank fire, armed with a newly developed 76mm gun and powered by V12 diesel engine. Stalin approved the design and named it the KV in honour of Marshal Klimenti Voroshilov who had been instrumental in developing the Russian tank industry. The 46-ton tank had armour up to 77mm thick, carried a crew of five and was to have many components – including the engine – in common with the T-34. The KV-1 entered service in 1939 and first saw action during the war against Finland when they were used in the final assault on the Mannerheim Line.

Contemporary reports suggest that KV series tanks were poorly designed ergonomically and difficult to drive. Nevertheless they were undoubtedly powerfully armed, rugged and able to withstand a considerable amount of punishment. There were several different versions produced: the KV-1A introduced in 1940 had an improved gun and new mantlet, the KV-1B introduced in 1941 had extra armour attached, and the KV-1C, introduced in 1942, had even thicker armour (up to 120mm), a cast turret, uprated engine and wider tracks. The KV-2A introduced in 1940 was a close-support version armed with a 152mm howitzer mounted in an enormous slab-sided turret which, together with armour up to 100mm thick, increased the vehicle's weigh to an unwieldy 53 tons. It proved to be of limited value.

KV-1s were built at the Kirovskiy Works in Leningrad until 1941 when the city came under threat and the factory was evacuated to Chelyabinsk – known as 'Tankograd'. There are currently no KV-1 or KV-2 tanks in running order. The KV-2 illustrated (**below**, courtesy of Fraser Gray) is on display in the grounds of the Central Armed Forces

Museum, Moscow, while the 1942-built KV-1 bearing the wartime Finnish swastika markings (**above**, courtesy of Fraser Gray) is preserved at Parola in Finland.

T-34

When first encountered in the summer of 1941 the T-34 came as a nasty surprise to the German Army. The only weapon they had to stop it was the 88mm anti-aircraft gun and they had no comparable tank. General Heinz Guderian's verdict that 'the T-34 was the best tank in any army up to 1943' said it all, and when German officers on the Eastern Front had recovered from their initial surprise at being faced by such an advanced tank, they seriously suggested that the best answer would be simply to copy the design.

In the early 1930s the Russians were much taken with the work of American tank designer J. Walter Christie who produced the T3, an innovative light tank capable of running at high speed on tracks or wheels. The Russians purchased two, copied them, and developed them into the BT series of

light tanks which stayed in production until 1940. Because of the increasing power of anti-tank weapons it was realised that what was really needed was a design which offered a compromise between speed and manoeuvrability on one hand, and armour protection and firepower on the other. So in 1938 they introduced the A-20 medium tank which retained the dual wheels or tracks characteristic of the BT series, but featured a radically sloped hull and turret almost identical to that which would later appear on the T-34.

The A-20 was still relatively lightly armoured and was only armed with a 45mm gun, but the next development, the T-32, ran on tracks only, was armed with a 76mm gun and had increased armour protection. In August 1938 the Supreme War Council approved the design for production and the T-34 was born. As an aside, the Russians were the first to develop a successful diesel tank engine although it is thought in the West that the V2 engine fitted to the T-34 and many other Russian tanks owed much to an earlier Italian design. Whatever the truth,

the engine was efficient, economical, reliable and powerful. On average the T-34 was capable of a little over 30mph and had an operational radius of about 280 miles. The Christie-type suspension gave it an excellent cross-country performance aided by 19in wide tracks; a feature which allowed the T-34 to negotiate soft ground or snow that would bog down any comparable German tank.

The first T-34 rolled off the line at Kharkov in June 1940. Production was also undertaken at Leningrad and Stalingrad, but as the Germans advanced on Leningrad and into the Ukraine, the Kharkov and Leningrad plants were moved to Chelyabinsk, east of the Urals, and were combined with the local tractor factory to form a massive tank production centre known as 'Tankograd'. The Stalingrad plant stayed put and, as the Germans besieged the city, T-34s were being driven straight off the production line and into combat. Early production models, known in the West as the T-34/76 because of their short 76.2mm gun, had a maximum armour thickness of 45mm and a two-man turret. In

1941, to counter the threat posed by new German anti-tank weapons, the T-34's hull armour was increased in thickness by 2mm and the turret armour increased to 60mm.

The T-34/76's two-man turret – wherein the tank commander/gunner sat on the right and the loader on the left – was particularly cramped. And in any case, it is debatable whether one man could fulfil both commander and gunner roles with any great success. So in December 1943 the T-34/85 emerged with an enlarged three-man turret. The new mark was armed with an 85mm gun said to be roughly equivalent to the German 88mm. Clearly the Russians had made a good tank even better. Not that it was without its faults. Little or no attention had been paid to crew comfort, the transmission was unreliable, the gearchange heavy, the steering system of a primitive clutch-and-brake type and the gun's fire control system more primitive than that utilised by Western tanks. Nevertheless, there can be little doubt that in general terms the T-34 was one of the best tanks of the Second World War.

The T-34 continued in production after the war in Soviet, Polish and Czech factories. It is hard to be precise as to the final build total, but it is estimated to have been in the region of 52,000. Large numbers were exported to countries sympathetic to the Soviet cause and, as a result, T-34s saw action from Korea to the Middle East. There are no T-34/76s still in running order although several are preserved in museums such as this slightly modified example in Finnish markings (**previous page, top**, courtesy of Fraser Gray) kept at the Parola Tank Museum in Finland. However, having only quite recently retired from active service many T-34/85s (**previous page, bottom and above**) have appeared on the private market. With so many having been built, spares are less of a problem than with many Western Second World War vintage AFVs.

SU-100 Self-propelled Gun

The SU-85 and SU-100 were intended to support infantry as either assault guns or tank destroyers. The advantage of such weapons is that they are simpler and therefore cheaper to produce than tanks, and can be armed with a more powerful gun than could be shoehorned into a turreted vehicle based on the same chassis. The SU-85 was based on the T-34 chassis and primarily conceived as a tank destroyer although its 85mm gun could also fire high-explosive rounds. By the time the SU-85 appeared in service in late 1943 heavier German tanks were being encountered on the battlefield, so it was decided to replace the 85mm gun with a more potent weapon. The 100mm gun mounted in the SU-100 had a good all-round performance although is said not to have had the penetration capability of the German long 75mm gun. However, at 34lb, the 100mm's AP projectile was almost twice the weight of that fired by the German weapon and could seriously damage any vehicle it hit whether or not penetration was achieved. The 100mm gun could also fire a 35lb high-explosive shell.

The SU series had several advantages over tanks apart from their simplicity of construction and ability to mount a heavier gun. They were of a remarkably low profile and therefore presented a much smaller target from all aspects. Also the lack of a turret avoided a so-called 'shot trap' between hull and turret (tanks are inclined to be vulnerable in that area as even a non-penetrative hit can damage the turret ring and prevent traverse). Also more ammunition could be carried internally. The obvious and major disadvantage was the gun's limited traverse, 20 degrees in the SU-85 and 16 degrees in the SU-100. Another potential problem was that the SU-100's gun could only be depressed 2 degrees which meant the crew would have to dig the front of the vehicle in if they needed to fire 'downhill'. It is probably true to say that the SU series were of more use in defence than in attack and as the tide of war turned in Russia's favour so production of tanks far exceeded that of SP guns. Total production

figures are unclear, but SU-100s were exported to East Germany, Poland, Czechoslovakia, Egypt, Hungary, Syria and Iraq , and served with the Russian Army into the 1970s. This example is maintained in running order at the Imperial War Museum (**above and right**).

IS-2 Heavy Tank

In 1943 a development of the KV series appeared mounting an 85mm gun and known as the IS-85 or IS-1 (Klimenti Voroshilov, Defence Commissar at the time of the German invasion, was by then out of favour so the new heavy tank was named after Ioseph (Joseph) Stalin). Only about 100 were built before an improved model mounting a 122mm gun and designated IS-2 went into full-scale production. About 2,250 were built and they first appeared in battle in the spring of 1944 as the Germans were being pushed back westwards. With well sloped and sculpted armour up to 160mm thick, the IS-2 had exceptionally

good ballistic protection. Couple that with the fact that its 122mm gun fired a shell with enough explosive to blow the turret off an enemy tank even if it did not penetrate its armour and it is clear that the IS-2 was more than a match for heavy German armour. The Imperial War Museum received the IS-2 shown (**above**, courtesy of Mark Ansell) in exchange for a Conqueror. The evocative shot of an IS-2 in faded parade markings (**below**, courtesy of Fraser Gray) was taken at Russia's famous Kubinka Museum.

IS-3 Heavy Tank

If the IS-2 was impressive then its successor, the 46-ton IS-3, was positively stunning. Introduced in 1945, its hull and turret were of a radically streamlined shape and low silhouette hitherto unseen. The IS-3 was still armed with the lethal 122mm D2 gun but its frontal armour was up to an almost impenetrable 200mm thick. Both the IS-2 and IS-3 were powered by similar 520hp V12 engines and capable of a 25mph top speed. On the face of it the IS-3 was an extremely formidable weapon, albeit a little cramped inside. It was only produced in limited numbers and was replaced in Soviet service by the T10 (IS-8) in the mid sixties. Although IS-3s took part in the 1945 Berlin Victory parade, the tank is thought not to have actually seen combat during the

Second World War. The vehicle shown (**above**, courtesy of Fraser Gray), an IS-3M probably rebuilt in 1959–60, was photographed close to the Great Patriotic War Museum just outside Moscow.

ISU-152

The ISU-152 was the heaviest calibre self-propelled gun to see action with the Russian Army during the Second World War. It was similar to the earlier KV series based SU-152, but utilised the IS series tank chassis after production of the KV-1 ceased in 1943. The massive ML-20 152mm howitzer could fire a 96lb high-explosive shell almost 9,000 metres and its 107lb armour-piercing shell could devastate any tank from long range.

The ISU-152 weighed 46 tons and its armour varied between 20 and 90mm thick. The rear-mounted V-12-IS diesel engine drove the rear sprockets via a four-speed gearbox and propelled the vehicle to a maximum speed of 23mph. This seemingly well preserved example (**right**, courtesy of Fraser Gray) was pictured near the Great Patriotic War Museum, Moscow.

PT-76

On only one occasion did US Army tanks directly do battle with NVA tanks during the Vietnam War. That was on 3 March 1969 when five M48 Pattons defended the Special Forces Camp at Ben Het from an attack by

eight PT-76s. Despite the difference in numbers it was an unfair contest and the heavier armed and armoured Pattons destroyed two of the PT-76s before the rest retreated. Nor did Egyptian PT-76s fare any better under Israeli fire when trying to cross

the Suez Canal during the Yom Kippur War in 1973. The fact is that although the amphibious PT-76 is a relatively large and imposing vehicle, it is of necessity thinly armoured.

The PT-76 entered service with the Soviet Army in 1952. Its boat-like hull (**above**) is constructed of welded armour no more than 14mm thick. The driver sits in the front while the commander/gunner and loader occupy the turret. The vehicle is powered by a V6 diesel engine and can attain a speed of about 27mph on the road. In amphibious mode two water jets exiting from the hull rear (**below**) can propel the PT-76 to a speed of 6mph. Three basic models were produced armed with marginally different 76.2mm guns. Model A had a long multi-slotted muzzle brake; Model 2, had a double baffle muzzle brake with bore evacuator, and Model 3 was as Model 2, but without a bore evacuator. All had a 7.62mm machine-gun mounted coaxially. Production ceased in the early 1960s, but the PT-76 has served with the armies of almost two dozen countries, so it is not uncommon in private hands (**top right**).

T-54/55

The T-54 was a development of the unsuccessful T-44 which was itself a descendant of the legendary T-34. The T-44 featured an improved torsion bar suspension system and ballistically better shaped hull and turret, but proved unreliable and was only produced in small numbers. Efforts to improve the T-44 resulted in the first proto-type T-54 emerging in 1947 with, among other things, a redesigned turret mounting a 100mm gun and a V12 water-cooled diesel engine and transmission mounted trans-versely at the rear.

By 1954 the T-54 had become the Soviets' standard medium tank and was continu-ously improved until re-designated the T-55 in the late 1950s. The T-54/55 has an all welded hull and cast turret. The driver sits in the left-hand front of the hull and the other three crew members occupy the turret. The T-54/55's turret is well shaped ballistically speaking, but in comparison with Western tanks is cramped and possesses a crude fire-control system. Nor can it rotate as fast as the turrets on contemporary Western tanks. For that reason alone the T-54/55 could be at a distinct disadvantage in a one to one contest. Nevertheless it has proved to be an extremely rugged and reliable tank and, although accurate production figures are unavailable, if you include Czech, Polish and Chinese (as the Types 59 and 69) produc-tion, it is likely that between 60,000 and 70,000 have been built.

The T-54/55 runs on torsion-bar type suspension with the drive sprocket at the front and idler at the rear. It can wade to a maximum depth of 4ft 7in without prepara-tion, but with the aid of a snorkel can ford rivers to a depth of 18ft. The T-55 differs in only relatively minor detail. Its engine is more powerful and it has an NBC system as standard. The T-54's 12.7mm anti-aircraft machine-gun was deleted, but subse-quently most T-55s had the gun retro-fitted. Both tanks were capable of a 30mph maximum speed and had an operational range of about 250 miles, although extra

fuel tanks could be attached to the rear hull if necessary.

The T-54/55 does not appear to have fared well in combat when faced with its Western counterparts, for instance in Syrian hands against Israeli armour during the Yom Kippur War of October 1973. But it would be unwise to draw too harsh a conclusion from such evidence. The T-54/55 is undoubtedly both competent and reliable and if the Syrians were at a disadvantage it was likely to have been as much a result of the Israeli tank crews' superior training and experience. The T-55 illustrated (**previous page and right**) is ex-East German Army and now owned by the Imperial War Museum.

T-62

The T-62 was developed in the late 1950s to succeed the T-54/55 series to which, at first glance, it appears quite similar. Probably the most obvious difference is that, unlike the T-54/55 which has a distinctive gap between its first and second roadwheels, the T-62's wheels are more evenly spaced. The T-62's hull is also marginally wider and longer and the turret of a slightly more

squat contour. The turret is, of course, of cast construction varying between 60mm and 170mm thick and the hull is of all welded construction. A 700bhp water-cooled V-2-62 12-cylinder engine gives the tank a similar performance to that of the T-54/55, but with a slightly greater range of about 280 miles.

The T-62 carries a crew of four: driver, commander, gunner and loader, but the 115mm U-5TS main gun – which fires high-explosive, fin-stabilised armour-piercing discarding sabot and high-explosive anti-tank rounds – is fitted with what amounts to a semi-automatic loading system. Rounds are loaded manually, but after firing the gun returns to a set angle so that the empty cartridge case can be ejected from the breech and disposed of through a hatch in the turret rear. Reports suggest that this system has proven unreliable. In addition to the main gun there is a coaxially mounted 7.62mm machine-gun, and many T-62s also have a 12.7mm anti-aircraft machine-gun mounted on the loader's cupola.

This particular T-62 (**bottom left**), recently acquired by the Imperial War Museum, is fitted with a snorkel erected over the loader's hatch. Without preparation or the aid of a snorkel a T-62 can ford to a depth of a little over 4ft, but with the maximum snorkel extensions fitted it can ford to a depth of 18ft.

T-72

A T-72 being put through its paces some-where east of the Urals? Actually no, it was photographed (**below**) while being displayed in the Imperial War Museum's arena at Duxford in Cambridgeshire. Such an event would have been inconceivable a few years ago, but with the ending of the Cold War and fleets of armour being made redundant on both sides of the old Iron Curtain almost anything is now possible.

When first seen in public in 1977, the T-72 (and parallel developed T-64) signalled the Soviet's departure from the Christie-type suspension favoured ever since the Second World War. The T-72 has six large road wheels with the drive sprocket at the rear and idler at the front plus three return rollers. Standard equipment includes an NBC system, night vision equipment and a snorkel for deep wading – a feature best demonstrated with the hatches shut (**over-**

leaf)! A 780hp diesel engine propels the T-72 to a spectacular maximum top speed of 50mph and gives it a range of about 300 miles. The main armament is a 125mm smoothbore gun able to fire APDS, HE and HEAT projectiles, and some 40 rounds can be carried internally. In a radical departure from the norm, the gun has an automatic reload system which means the T-72 only requires a three-man crew. Additional armament consists of a coaxially mounted 7.62mm machine-gun and a 12.7mm anti-aircraft machine-gun mounted by the commander's cupola.

Although the T-72 is undoubtedly fast and manoeuvrable, combat experience has raised questions about the design. For instance, when Syrian T-72s clashed with Israeli armour in Lebanon, observers are said to have noted a propensity for internal ammunition fires – a tank crew's worst nightmare. Whether or not that is the case, Gulf War experience certainly called into doubt the practicality of the T-72's auto-load system. After every round fired by Iraqi T-72s it was observed that the system caused their guns to be taken off target and auto-matically elevated to the reload position.

pivot turn. The T-72 won't do that. It has to be in gear so you always have some forward or backward motion.'

The gear change is also a little odd. They found that the clutch is needed to get in and out of first gear, but from then on gear changes are clutchless. Whereas, when driving the world's largest tracked vehicle, the 2S7 self-propelled gun, which is supposed to have – and certainly appears to have – the same engine and transmission as the T-72, they found that it was necessary always to use the clutch. 'Is there something wrong or are they completely different systems,' ponders Hutcheson. 'We don't have the full technical manuals so unless we take them apart to find out how they work it's a problem. Sometimes with Russian vehicles it's a case of suck it and see.'

2S3 (M-1973) 152mm Self-propelled Howitzer

Up until the introduction of the 2S3 'Akat-siya' (Acacia) in the early 1970s, the Soviets had relied almost entirely on towed artillery. The vehicle's general layout is similar to that of the American M109 which was introduced some ten years earlier. The driver sits alongside the 520hp V12 diesel at the front and a 152mm gun/howitzer (developed from the towed 152mm D-20), fitted with a double baffle brake and fume extractor, is mounted in a large turret at the rear. The gun is said to be capable of firing a 96lb high-explosive projectile to a maximum range of over 26,000 yards and, using a 107lb armour-piercing round, penetrate 5in of armour at a range of 1,000 yards. The turret can be traversed through a full 360 degrees and the gun elevated +56 degrees and –3 degrees. Around 40 projectiles can be carried internally and there is a re-supply hatch at the rear (**top right**). Unlike the M109 there are no spades fitted to the hull rear to help absorb recoil.

2S3s were exported to Bulgaria, the GDR, Hungary, Libya, Syria and Iraq, who unwillingly donated this (**bottom right and overleaf**) example, the only 2S3 in running order in the UK, to the Imperial War Museum after the Gulf War. Many of the Russian-built vehicles exported to Arab

They were unable continuously to track their prey between shots, and in the 12 seconds it took to raise the T-72's gun and reload, the American Abrams was capable of firing two rounds. Of course the T-72 is neither as well armed nor as well armoured as the Challenger and Abrams, and its main advantage, speed, was negated by the Iraqis frequently using them dug-in to static defensive positions.

What's it like to drive? 'Interesting,' says Andy Hutcheson, chairman of Duxford's Vehicle Wing and one of only a couple of drivers experienced enough to handle the T-72. 'The whole concept of the vehicle is different. Even the Russian way of steering is different. With the Chieftain you just hold the steering levers and away you go. But the T-72 has three or four different lever positions for varying degrees of turn. And if you pull the levers right back you disengage drive completely. Nor will it neutral steer. You can put the Chieftain in neutral, rev it up, pull back the steering lever and do a

countries have their instruments and controls labelled in English. This particular vehicle was an exception, but since the control layout followed the usual Soviet practice IWM personnel had no great problem working out what did what. Like T-34s and T-54/55s, etc., the 2S3 has a steel plated clutch which, if operated as if it were a British tank or car clutch, i.e., slipped, will overheat and warp. The correct procedure to get into gear is to pull the 2S3's steering levers fully back to disengage drive, depress the clutch pedal, engage first gear, let up the clutch, and then move the steering levers forward to re-engage drive. While experimenting, Duxford Vehicle Wing members unexpectedly found that, unlike other Russian tracked vehicles, the 2S3 would neutral steer, i.e., pirouette on the spot.

2S7 Self-propelled 207mm Gun

At 42ft in length, the massive 2S7 is said to be the world's largest tracked armoured vehicle. It is thought to have entered service with the Soviet Army in the mid-eighties. The 203mm gun is capable of firing nuclear ammunition and is quoted as having a range of 30kms. Believe it or not this particular example (**below**) was purchased from the Czech Army on behalf of an American collector and is pictured at the Imperial War Museum where it made a brief appearance while in transit.

GERMANY

SdKfz 251 Half-track

In the mid-thirties when the German Army were formulating tactics that would later become known as 'Blitzkrieg', they identified a need for an armoured troop carrying vehicle with similar cross-country ability to that of a tank. The half-track seemed the ideal solution and there were already a number of soft-skin half-tracks in service or under development for the purpose of towing heavy artillery. It was the chassis of one of these, the Hanomag Hkl 6 three-ton tractor, that served as the basis for the SdKfz (Sonderkraftfahrzeug = special-purpose vehicle) 251 series (**below**). Production started in 1939 and continued throughout the war in four basic marks and a comprehensive range of specialised variants.

The hull was composed of well sloped, mainly welded armour plates 14.5mm thick at the front and 8mm thick at the sides. In its basic form the vehicle accommodated a ten-man infantry squad on two benches facing a central aisle at the rear (**overleaf, top**) plus a driver and commander. The Ausf A, B and C were very similar in appearance except that the Ausf C had a flat plate nose. The Ausf D featured a modified superstructure with simplified lines and flat plate rear doors rather than the distinctive 'clam shell' doors of its predecessors.

Manoeuvring the vehicles was via a steering wheel in the orthodox manner, but the steering box had two arms: one to the front axle and the other to track brakes mounted on each side of the differential. Weighing in at a little under eight tons, the SdKfz 251 had a top speed of 33mph and a fuel consumption of about three miles to the gallon. The list of specialised variants extends to almost two dozen including 37mm or 75mm anti-tank gun armed versions, several radio vehicles, an ambulance and a flame-thrower unit. With around 15,000 SdKfz 251s having been produced, it must rank as the most numerous German AFV of the Second World War.

Some had been built in Czech factories, and post-war the SdKfz 251 continued in Czech Army service. In the 1950s the

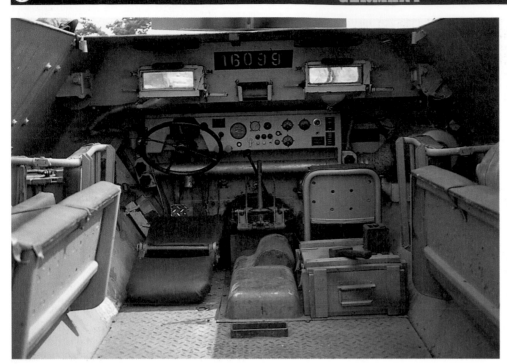

Czechs decided to put into production their own modified version. The resulting Skoda/Tatra OT-810 was closely patterned on the German vehicle, but had roof armour, a Tatra V8 air-cooled diesel engine (**right**) and easy maintenance dry-pin tracks. Around 1,500 were manufactured between 1959 and 1963. Many of these became surplus to requirements in the 1980s and were sold off. Those that have since passed into the hands of collectors have been converted closely to resemble the original German vehicle (**below left and right**).

PzKpfw II

Under the terms of the Treaty of Versailles Germany was not allowed to possess armoured fighting vehicles. Nevertheless, throughout the 1930s they rebuilt their

armoured forces. At first they did this surreptitiously, but as Hitler came to power it became more open.

In 1934 development contracts were issued to Krupp, Henschel and MAN for a 10-ton tank to have thicker armour and a larger gun than the earlier PzKpfw I. After the designs had been assessed MAN were chosen to take charge of chassis development with Daimler-Benz looking after the superstructure and turret. The project was allotted the misleading code name of 'LaS 100' – LaS standing for Landwirtschaftlicher Schlepper or agricultural tractor. Through 1936 and early 1937 small batches of development models were produced, each incorporating improvements to such areas as engine cooling, tracks and, notably, the suspension which evolved from one similar to that used by the PzKpfw I to one featuring

five independently sprung road wheels with four return rollers.

The Ausf A entered production in July 1937, followed by the externally identical Ausf B in December 1937 and the Ausf C in June 1938. They weighed a little under nine tons, had armour between 5mm and 15mm thick and were armed with a 2cm KwK 30 main gun and 7.92mm MG34 machine-gun. With power from a 135hp Maybach engine the top speed was 25mph with a range of about 125 miles.

The Ausf D and E were introduced in 1938 with a radically different torsion bar suspension and four, rather than five, road wheels. They were also fitted with a more powerful engine which gave them a much enhanced top speed of 35mph. Less than 50 of these versions, known as the Schnellkampfwagen (fast fighting vehicle) were built. The last production version, the Ausf F, was introduced in 1941. It was armed with a 2cm KwK L/55 main gun and had

thicker armour than earlier marks, but was otherwise similar. The Ausf F illustrated (**above**, courtesy of Panzermuseum Münster) was captured in Libya and put on display at the Aberdeen Proving Grounds. In 1989 it was handed over to the Panzermuseum Münster on long term loan in return for it's being restored. It is now in full running order.

After the Ausf F there were several small development batches produced featuring various modifications, but none went into full-scale production. The PzKpfw II chassis was also used as the basis for several self-propelled guns, a bridgelayer and a flame-thrower. In the early Blitzkrieg years the PzKpfw II contributed greatly to the Germans' success but its vulnerability became more apparent as the war progressed. By early 1942 it was relegated to reconnaissance duties and was then gradually phased out until completely disappearing from front-line service in 1943.

PzKpfw III

By the mid-thirties Germany had come to realise that it would be unrealistic for their new panzer divisions to rely on just two basic types of tank. In addition to a fast, lightweight tank armed with a 2cm gun, and a medium tank with thicker armour capable of infantry support (which evolved as the PzKpfw II and IV respectively), something between the two was needed. Development contracts for the new tank were issued in 1935. It was expected to have a similar layout to the PzKpfw IV and be armed with a 37mm gun, the standard infantry anti-tank gun of the period. In a concession to General Guderian who had wanted the new tank to mount a 50mm gun, it was agreed that the new design would incorporate a turret ring of sufficient diameter to allow for the mounting of heavier weapons at a later date.

The PzKpfw III as we know it today evolved from a series of Daimler-Benz designs, known at the time as the 1/ZW,

2/ZW, 3a/ZW and 3b/ZW. Each had a different suspension system and it wasn't until the 4/ZW that the designers hit upon a successful layout using six pairs of torsion-bar supported road wheels. Only very small numbers of the earlier attempts had been produced, but 100 4/ZW, or PzKpfw III Ausf E, were manufactured. In September 1939 the Ausf F entered production by which time it was realised that Guderian had been right to demand a more powerful gun for the new tank. The 50mm gun was not immediately available so most Ausf Fs were built still armed with the 35mm weapon. It wasn't until the AusfG that the 50mm KwK L/42 was fitted as standard.

Subsequent marks, Ausf H through M, incorporated various modifications including an improved transmission, re-designed turret and thicker armour. The Ausf J was the most numerous of the different marks with 2,616 being produced, the last 1,000 or so being armed with a new long-barrelled L/60 gun as were the Ausf L and M. The final mark, the Ausf N, went into production early in 1943 and was fitted with

a 75mm KwK L/24 short-barrelled gun which was better suited to the infantry support role to which the PzKpfw III had by then been relegated.

The 1942-built Ausf L photographed (**previous page, top**) at the Tank Museum's annual 'Battle Day' was captured in Libya during the Second World War, whereas the camouflaged vehicle – a hybrid Ausf M hull with Ausf L turret (**previous page, bottom above and above right**) – was recovered from Norway in 1997. In fact only relatively minor modifications such as a higher mounted exhaust for better wading capability differentiate the Ausf L and M.

StuG III

One of the most successful dual role anti-tank/assault vehicles developed by Germany during the Second World War was the Sturmgeschütze (StuG) III. In fact they are said to have destroyed more tanks than the PzKpfw III on which they were based. Not only that, the StuG III was cheaper to produce and, being of a lower profile, easier

to conceal on the battlefield. When introduced in 1940 they were armed with a short-barrel 75mm StuK37 L/24 gun, but with the introduction of the Ausf F in 1941 came the more powerful 75mm StuK40 L/43 long-barrelled gun. The Ausf F8 and Ausf G, the last production version, were both armed with the improved L/48 version of the same gun. With its new long-barrelled gun the StuG III became lethally effective in any role. Weighing between 20 and 24 tons and with a crew of four, the vehicle's 12-cylinder Maybach engine gave the StuG III a maximum speed of almost 25mph.

At the end of the war most of the survivors of the 8,000+ built were scrapped or used as targets on firing ranges. But a few survived to serve with the Spanish Army until the mid-fifties, when some were sold on to Syria, and a number remained in Finnish Army service until the mid-sixties. One such is the example illustrated (**right**). It was built by Alkett in Berlin and was one of ten shipped to Finland in 1943. The Finns used it against the Russians during the 'Continuation War' and the vehicle stayed in

service with the Finnish Army until 1966. When purchased from the Finnish Ministry of Defence by its current owner in 1994, three sets of faded markings were visible; the German cross, Finnish swastika and post-war Finnish blue and white roundel. By 1996 all had been obliterated by a coat of dunkelgelb, the sand-yellow adopted as the basic colour for all German vehicles in all theatres from February 1943 onwards. Photographed a year later (**left**) the vehicle had gained an over-spray of green faithfully duplicating the practice of applying camouflage in the field. Note the Ausf G's superstructure is slightly wider than preceding marks and extends over the tracks. Also note that this early production Ausf G has a box-type gun mantlet. From 1944 onwards most Ausf Gs came with a cast mantlet known as a Saukopfblende (sow's head mount) because of its shape as typified by the example preserved in working order by the Panzermuseum Münster (**bottom left**, courtesy of Panzermuseum Münster).

This StuG III looks particularly effective laden with weekend panzergrenadiers from one of the UK's leading battle enactment groups (**below**). The appearance of armed

troops – particularly Third Reich troops – at military vehicle shows occasionally prompts adverse comment. The Invicta Military Vehicle Preservation Society, at whose annual show the StuG III was photographed, are careful to ensure that such displays are in the context of living history and in no way either glorify war or celebrate unacceptable ideologies.

PzKpfw IV

It is probably fair to say that the PzKpfw IV has been overshadowed by its heavier and more charismatic brethren the Tiger and Panther. The latter were undoubtedly fine fighting machines, but the PzKpfw IV remained in production throughout the Second World War and, with the PzKpfwIII, both established the reputation of Germany's armoured forces and formed its backbone.

Development commenced in 1934 on a vehicle armed with a 75mm assault gun to complement the new PzKpfw III which was to carry a 37mm gun. The vehicle's weight could not exceed 24 tons because that was the maximum capacity of a standard road bridge of the time. A Krupp design was

accepted in 1936 and a few PzKpfw IV Ausf (Ausführung) As came off their Magdeburg production line that same year. The second version, Ausf B, appeared in 1937 and Ausf C and D emerged in 1938. Because the PzKpfw IV was only intended to equip the fourth company of a standard tank battalion it was produced in limited numbers and only 211 were available when the Germans invaded Poland in 1939. Nevertheless results in battle were encouraging.

The Ausf F introduced in 1940 drew on combat experience and had thicker armour but the biggest improvement came with the Ausf F2. At the time the PzKpfw IV was the only tank the Germans had capable of being up-armoured and up-gunned and, in an attempt to counter the Russian T-34, the Ausf F2 mounted a long barrel, high-velocity 75mm gun. Small numbers of the up-gunned tank appeared in 1942 on the Eastern Front and in North Africa and had an immediate effect. Guderian became a particular fan of the type but his attempts to have production increased were constantly thwarted by others who diverted PzKpfw IV production from tanks to assault guns. Nevertheless PzKpfw IV production did continue right to

the bitter end of the war by which time some 9,000 had been manufactured. The vehicle illustrated (**above**, courtesy of Fraser Gray) is actually a command tank, or Panzerbefehlswagen, one of only 97 converted for this purpose in 1944, and is kept at the Brussels Tank Museum.

Hummel Self-propelled Gun

Plans to produce a single tank based upon PzKpfw III and IV components reached the prototype stage but were abandoned in 1944. However the PzKpfw III/IV chassis was used for a range of self-propelled guns. One such was the Hummel (Bumble Bee) which mounted a 15cm sFH18/1 L30 heavy howitzer and entered service late 1943. The 24-ton vehicle accommodated a crew of six, but could only carry 18 rounds of ammunition internally, so an unarmed version was produced as an ammunition carrier.

The vehicle illustrated (**top right**, courtesy of Panzermuseum Münster) was captured by American troops late in the war and shipped back to the United States. In 1976 it was donated by the Patton Museum in Kentucky to the Panzermuseum Münster. It was restored in Germany and is thought to be the only example in running order.

PzKpfw VI Tiger

The Tiger's complicated lineage can be traced back to 1937 when Henschel were instructed to design an infantry tank of between 30 and 33 tons weight armed with a 75mm howitzer and designated DW1 (DW= Durchbruchswagen, or breakthrough tank). A year later design effort was switched to a prospective 65-ton tank which was subsequently shelved after two prototypes had been built. Henschel then returned to the DW1 project and produced in 1940 an improved DW2 design mounting the 75mm L/24 howitzer. There was yet another change of course when the specification was amended to include the long-barrelled 75mm L/48 and three other companies, Porsche, MAN and Daimler-Benz, entered

the competition. The VK3001, as the project was known, did not get beyond the prototype stage. At much the same time the companies were also working on a 36-ton tank project designated VK3601 which was to feature a high-velocity gun, thick armour and a top speed of 25mph.

Henschel finished a prototype VK3601 before, yet again, the project was cancelled, this time in favour of VK4501 which was to mount a version of the deadly 88mm FlaK gun. The order for VK4501 was placed in May 1941 and Hitler demanded that the prototypes be ready for demonstration on his next birthday, 20 April 1942. Both Henschel and Porsche met the deadline by incorporating the best features of their VK3001 and VK3601 designs into the new VK4501. As decreed, the competing tanks were demonstrated in front of Hitler on 20 April at Rastenburg and the Henschel design was subsequently judged superior. A production order was placed and the new tank designated the PzKpfw VI Tiger Ausf E.

GERMANY

115

The design wasn't ideal for mass production. It took 300,000 man hours to build just one Tiger so only 1,350 were delivered between August 1942 and August 1944 with production never exceeding 104 in a month. That aside, it was an outstanding design. The hull and super-structure were constructed from large armour plates incorporating steps at the joints which acted as seats for the welds. The Tiger was the first German tank to be equipped with an overlapping road wheel suspension consisting of three rows of interleaved steel wheels for optimum weight distribution. Two different widths of track could be fitted: 28$^{1}/_{2}$ in wide for combat and good cross-country performance and, with the outer row of wheels removed, 21in wide for transport. The original 21litre Maybach V12 engine left the 57-ton Tiger under-powered so was replaced from December 1943 with a 24litre HL 230 P45 engine. Both were coupled to a Maybach pre-selector gearbox with eight forward and four reverse ratios.

The 1st SS Panzer Division Liebstandarte 'Adolf Hitler' and the 2nd SS Panzer Division 'Das Reich' were the first units to receive the Tiger. Perhaps fortunately for the Allies, Tigers were never available in any great numbers so did not have the impact in attack that such a formidable weapon would other-wise have had. It is probably true to say that it proved its worth more in defence. Able to destroy any Allied tank with its 88mm gun and, because of its 100mm armour, all but impervious to frontal assault, one strategi-cally placed Tiger could – and frequently did – seriously hinder the Allied advance. The only hope for an Allied tank was to approach from the side or rear and close to a range of under 700 yards. A dangerous enterprise because the Tiger's 20lb tungsten-cored armour-piercing shot could destroy a Sherman from twice that distance.

A handful of Tigers survive in reasonable condition, such as this example at the Panz-ermuseum, Münster (**previous page**, courtesy of Panzermuseum Münster), but there are none in private hands and none, as yet, in running condition. However, the Tank Museum at Bovington are working on restoring their example, captured in Tunisia in April 1943, to full working order.

PzKpfw V Panther

Having presumed – with good reason – that their tanks were superior to anything they were likely to encounter on the battlefield, the German Army were, to say the least, surprised by the T-34. General Guderian requested that a team of tank design and production experts be sent to the Eastern Front so that they could examine captured and damaged T-34s and assess first-hand what needed to be done to counter the threat it posed. This they did in November 1941. Suggestions that they should simply take a T-34 and copy it were judged imprac-tical, but as a result of the visit specifica-tions for a new heavy tank were issued to Daimler-Benz and MAN.

The MAN design was approved with minor alterations to the turret and after successful testing was put into limited

production in November 1942 as the PzKpfw V Panther Ausf A. From January 1943 full mass production of the Ausf D commenced. Inexplicably the model that followed the Ausf D was designated Ausf A at which time the pre-production Ausf As were re-designated Ausf D1 and the original Ausf Ds re-designated Ausf D2. The most obvious difference between the Ausf A and Ausf D1/D2 was that the new model had its bow machine-gun mounted in a ball-mount. The final production model was the Ausf G which incorporated various minor modifications and one major one in that the hull sides were set at a steeper angle to increase interior space.

The Panther was armed with the formidable new 75mm L/70 gun designed by Rheinmetall-Borsig, and two 7.92mm MG34 machine-guns. Despite it being possible to build two Panthers in the time it would take to build one Tiger, MAN were unable to cope with a production target of 600 tanks per month. Therefore Daimler-Benz, Henschel and MNH all switched to Panther produc-

tion. The Panther had a five-man crew and was powered by a 12-cylinder Maybach engine that could take the 45-ton vehicle to a top speed of 29mph. Its armour, steeply sloped to emulate the T-34, varied between 15mm and 120mm thick. Having been rushed into service it was almost inevitable that the Panther would initially be plagued with problems. And so it turned out. During their first major engagement, of the 200 Panthers employed only 60 remained serviceable at the end of the day. In time the bugs were ironed out and various modifications made to the point where the final production model, the Ausf G, was considered by many to be the best tank of the war.

There are currently several Panthers preserved in working order, albeit rarely exhibited as such, and at least one – an Ausf A – is undergoing restoration in the UK. The vehicle illustrated (**below left and below**, courtesy of Bob Fleming) belongs to the Panzermuseum, Münster and, as can be seen from the extra aerials carried, is a command tank based on a Panther Ausf A.

Jagdpanther

When in 1942 the German Army needed a fast tank destroyer able to mount the fearsome 88mm PaK 43/4 L/71 anti-aircraft gun what better basis could there have been than the Panther. Maschinenfabrik Neidersachsen-Hannover developed a prototype which was demonstrated to, and approved by, Hitler in October 1943, and production commenced in January 1944. A well sloped, thickly armoured (up to 80mm) superstructure able to mount the chosen weapon was formed by the simple expedient of extending the Panther's existing hull side and front plates upwards at a steeper angle of 40 degrees.

The main gun had an elevation of –8 to +14 degrees and a limited traverse of 13 degrees left and right so it was quite normal for the entire vehicle to have to move to bring the gun to bear. The gun's recommended engagement range is said to have been 2,700 yards so it almost goes without saying that in a head to head confrontation the Jagdpanther could knock out any Allied tank without

endangering itself. The engine and running gear were the same as the Panther's so it had an excellent cross-country performance and creditable top speed, for a vehicle weighing 46 tons, of 29mph. Undoubtedly the Jagdpanther was a fearsomely efficient weapon, but only 392 were constructed before the war ended. The Jagdpanther emerging from the bushes (**above**, courtesy of Bob Fleming) is also part of the Panzermuseum Münster's fine collection.

PzKpfw VI Tiger II

The Tiger II, or PzKpfw VI Ausf B Königstiger (King Tiger), was the biggest and heaviest tank to see action during the Second World War. Weighing in at around 69 tons, 13ft 9in long and 12ft 4in wide, the Tiger II was, as might be expected, a cumbersome beast, although with Germany very much on the defensive mobility was not necessarily a major consideration at the time.

In August 1942 both Henschel and Porsche were invited to submit designs for a heavy tank mounting the new long-barrelled 88mm L/71 gun. Porsche submitted two designs. The first was simply a heavier version of their unsuccessful Tiger I design and was rejected in favour of their second design, a front engined tank with electric transmission. However, a severe shortage of copper, necessary in some quantity for the new transmission, led to the cancellation of Porsche's second design and once again Henschel won the day. A small consolation to Porsche was that fifty turrets that they had built (of a rather more streamlined shape than Henschel's version) were fitted to early production Tiger IIs.

The prototype appeared late 1943 and production ran from January 1944 to March 1945 in which time less than 500 were built. The Tiger II's 700hp Maybach HL230P30 engine, the same as that fitted to the

Panther Ausf G, drove the front sprockets via an eight-speed forward and four-speed reverse pre-selector gearbox and controlled differential. With hindsight the engine was not powerful enough for such a heavy vehicle and although its maximum road speed was a fairly respectable 20mph, cross-country and manoeuvring performance was poor and at worst fuel consumption is said to have been around 2½ gallons per mile.

However, the Allies had nothing to compare with the Tiger II in the areas of firepower and protection. 185mm of frontal armour made it impregnable to most Allied tanks while its incomparable 88mm gun could penetrate 80mm of armour at an amazing 4,000 metres and 200mm of armour at 1,000 metres. Tiger IIs first saw action on the Eastern Front and in Normandy and the Ardennes. Although the Tiger II Ausf B belonging to the Panzermu-

seum, Münster, (**above**, courtesy of Panzer-museum Münster) was restored to running order in 1982 it is thought that the only Tiger II currently driven with any regularity (although extremely infrequently) is the example preserved at Saumur in France.

Hetzer

The German Army were not slow to utilise captured vehicles or production facilities. In particular they impounded civilian trucks to service ever-lengthening supply chains and mounted a variety of guns on obsolete French and Czech tracked chassis. The Jagdpanzer 38(t) Hetzer (Baiter) was built by Praga and Skoda in Czechoslovakia using many components of their PzKpfw 38(t) tank which had itself been produced primarily for the German Army. It was of simple basic design with the four-man crew housed in a steeply raked hull constructed of welded armour plate of between 30mm and 60mm

thickness. The 75mm gun was mounted offset to the right to make room for the driver's compartment and had a very limited traverse, so frequently the entire vehicle had to be turned to bring the gun to bear. Many Hetzers had a remotely controlled machine-gun fitted to the hull roof. The vehicle was powered by a rear mounted Praga AC/2 six-cylinder engine and was capable of up to 25mph with an operational range of about 100 miles.

Between 1944 and 1945 over 2,500 Hetzers were manufactured. In 1946 the production line reopened to cater for an order from the Swiss Army for 158 of an updated version known as the G-13.

Improvements included replacing the original gun with a 75mm StuK 40 (with a muzzle brake) as used by the StuG III, and fitting a Saurer diesel engine in place of the old Czech unit. They remained in Swiss service into the 1970s when the remaining vehicles were disposed of. About two dozen still exist in private collections, many of them in running order (**previous page, bottom, left, top and bottom**) and reworked to resemble the original Second World War vehicle.

Leopard 1

When the West German Army re-equipped in 1955 the bulk of their AFV fleet was of US

manufacture. However, to help rebuild German industry and to further the interests of NATO commonality – a popular theory of the time – it was proposed that Germany, France and Italy work together to produce a 'Europanzer' and draft specifications were published in 1956. The two German design consortia: Team A, led by Porsche and Team B, led by Ruhrstal, produced two prototypes each in 1961. All four shared the same multi-fuel engine, a Daimler-Benz 838, and the same turret. Comparative tests came out in favour of Team A's designs and an order for twenty-six of the A-2 models was placed. As development continued the original 90mm

Rheinmetall gun was replaced by a 105mm gun from the same manufacturer and, finally, by the British Vickers L7A3 105mm gun which required a redesign of the turret. As is sometimes the way with such projects, the Italians dropped out completely and the French decided to put their own AMX-30 design into production, so leaving the Germans to continue on their own.

In October 1962 the new German tank was officially named as Leopard and shortly thereafter a production contract was awarded to Krauss-Maffei of Munich. The first production Leopard emerged in September 1965. Total production between then and 1979 amounted to 4,561 tanks of which 920 were built under licence by Oto Melara for the Italian Army. It proved to be an outstanding tank. Early comparative tests between Leopard and the AMX-30 revealed that the German design had a higher combat weight, better cross-country performance, was faster, and could fire three different types of round to the French tank's (at the time) one.

Leopard was subsequently sold to Australia, Canada, Belgium, Italy, the Netherlands, Denmark, Norway, Greece and Turkey.

This particular example (**previous page and below**), owned by the Tank Museum at Bovington, was originally obtained for trials in exchange for a Chieftain. On the road a Leopard is capable of an astonishing 40mph and although it could only attain a fraction of that in the display arena, it was able to demonstrate clearly its agility and superior acceleration.

MISCELLANEOUS

Strv m/40 – Sweden
This rare Strv m/40 (**below and overleaf, top**), owned and maintained in running order by the Tank Museum, is of particular interest because of its historical context. That its lines are reminiscent of early German light tank designs can be no surprise because it is a product of Lands-werk AB, an affiliate of the German Krupp company. With Germany theoretically prevented from re-arming by the Treaty of Versailles, Krupp set up Landswerk in Sweden and throughout the 1930s produced a range of wheeled and tracked armoured fighting vehicles. They were quite advanced designs and the invaluable development experience was passed back to the home-land and to the Russians with whom Germany was secretly collaborating on tank design at the time. The Strv m/40 weighed 11 tons, was armed with a 37mm main gun and two machine-guns and carried a crew of three. Sweden was a neutral country and their tank forces saw no action.

VT-34 Armoured Recovery Vehicle – Czechoslovakia

Although this Czech-designed and built VT-34 ARV looks for all the world like a converted SU-85 or SU-100 self-propelled gun, it is actually thought to be based on a T-34 tank. Signs of the conversion, only apparent when viewed from the interior, lead Duxford's Vehicle Wing – who operate the vehicle – to believe that it was probably a 1950s built T-34 converted in the early 1960s (**left and above**). Three were imported into the UK several years ago and one has since been shipped to America.

Praga V3S – Czechoslovakia

Many different versions of the Praga V3S three-ton 6x6 truck have been produced since the early fifties including these two: an armoured cargo truck and the M53 self-propelled twin 30mm anti-aircraft gun carrier. Both of the illustrated examples (**overleaf**) came from surplus Czech Army stocks.

AMX.13 – France

At the end of the Second World War the French Army was equipped almost entirely with American armour, but in 1946 the French Government set about re-equipping with French vehicles. Three AFVs were originally projected: the eight-wheeled Panhard EBR 75/10 armoured car; the AMX-50 main battle tank and the AMX-13 airportable light tank. Because of financial constraints the AMX-50 did not reach the production stage, but in any case the French Army, because of its involvement in colonial conflicts where the 'enemy' had no armour of its own, had a more pressing need for light tanks. However, the need for the AMX-13 to be airportable was somewhat academic in that

neither the French, or anyone else for that matter, had a transport aircraft capable of airlifting such a vehicle. That aspect aside, the AMX-13 was an extremely successful design, all the more remarkable for the radical features that were incorporated.

Prototypes were ready by 1949 and the AMX-13 went into production in 1952. It featured an oscillating turret and an automatic loader. Unlike conventional turrets, the AMX-13's consists of two basic components. The lower part is fixed to the turret

ring and supports, on two trunnions, the upper part which accommodates the gun, autoloader, commander and gunner. The gun is in a fixed mount and is elevated and depressed by moving the entire top part of the turret. One particular advantage of such a set-up is that it simplifies the design of an autoloader in that the gun and automatic load mechanism are always in the same relative position. It is also the case that the gun can be mounted very close to the turret roof which has the effect

of reducing the vehicle's overall height. Compactness was obviously a major factor when the AMX-13 was on the drawing board because it was specifically designed for crew members not exceeding 5ft 8in in height.

The AMX-13's autoloader is housed in the turret bustle and consists of two revolving cylinders, each holding six rounds of ammunition, one on each side of the gun breech recoil path. Recoil causes the cylinders to revolve and drop a round into the path of the breech into which it is automatically loaded. Empty cartridge cases are ejected through a hole in the rear of the bustle. Replenishment of the two ammunition cylinders can only be accomplished from the outside via hatches in the turret roof, a task which necessitates at least one crew member exposing himself to potential danger. On the plus side twelve rounds can be fired in very quick succession and the AMX-13 only requires a three-man crew.

Originally AMX-13s were armed with a 75mm gun based on the German L70 design fitted to Panther tanks, but the French Army later fitted a 90mm gun capable of firing fin-stabilised rounds. There was also a 105mm armed version built for export. A 7.5mm or 7.62mm machine-gun was fitted coaxially. A combat ready AMX-13 weighed less than 15 tons, but with armour nowhere thicker than 40mm did not offer particularly good protection for its crew. However, as might

be expected, it is highly manoeuvrable with a top road speed of 37mph and has an excellent cross-country performance. The engine is a SOFAM 8Gxb eight-cylinder unit driving the front sprockets via a manual five-speed and reverse gearbox.

Production of the AMX-13 gun tank ceased in 1964, but construction of the large range of variants continued long after that date. In all over 10,000 AMX-13 based vehicles were manufactured with a diversity only matched by the M113 family.

The AMX-13 was exported to over two dozen foreign countries and it has seen plenty of action, notably with the Israeli Army. The AMX-13 illustrated (**above and below**) was photographed while awaiting auction.